CliffsNotes

A Midsummer Night's Dream

By Karin Jacobson, Ph.D.

IN THIS BOOK

- Learn about the Life and Background of the Author
- Preview an Introduction to the Play
- Study a graphical Character Map
- Explore themes and literary devices in the Critical Commentaries
- Examine in-depth Character Analyses
- Enhance your understanding of the work with Critical Essays
- Reinforce what you learn with CliffsNotes Review
- Find additional information to further your study in CliffsNotes Resource Center and online at www.cliffsnotes.com

Wiley Publishing, Inc.

About the Author

Karin Jacobson received her Ph.D. in English from Ohio State University and is currently an Assistant Professor of English and Composition at the University of Minnesota-Duluth.

Publisher's Acknowledgments

Editorial

Project Editor: Tracy Barr

Acquisitions Editor: Greg Tubach

Glossary Editors: The editors and staff at Webster's New World™ Dictionaries

Editorial Administrator: Michelle Hacker

Production

Indexer: York Produnction Services, Inc.

Proofreader: York Produnction Services, Inc.

Wiley Publishing, Inc., Indianapolis Composition Services

CliffsNotes™ *A Midsummer Night's Dream*

Published by:
Wiley Publishing, Inc.
909 Third Avenue
New York, NY 10022
www.wiley.com

Table of Contents

How to Use This Book

CliffsNotes *A Midsummer Night's Dream* supplements the original work, giving you background information about the author, an introduction to the novel, a graphical character map, critical commentaries, expanded glossaries, and a comprehensive index. CliffsNotes Review tests your comprehension of the original text and reinforces learning with questions and answers, practice projects, and more. For further information on William Shakespear and *A Midsummer Night's Dream*, check out the CliffsNotes Resource Center.

CliffsNotes provides the following icons to highlight essential elements of particular interest:

Reveals the underlying themes in the work.

Helps you to more easily relate to or discover the depth of a character.

Uncovers elements such as setting, atmosphere, mystery, passion, violence, irony, symbolism, tragedy, foreshadowing, and satire.

Enables you to appreciate the nuances of words and phrases.

Don't Miss Our Web Site

Discover classic literature as well as modern-day treasures by visiting the CliffsNotes Web site at www.cliffsnotes.com. You can obtain a quick download of a CliffsNotes title, purchase a title in print form, browse our catalog, or view online samples.

You'll also find interactive tools that are fun and informative, links to interesting Web sites, tips, articles, and additional resources to help you, not only for literature, but for test prep, finance, careers, computers, and Internet too. See you at www.cliffsnotes.com!

LIFE AND BACKGROUND OF THE AUTHOR

Personal Background

William Shakespeare was born in 1564 in Stratford-upon-Avon, England, a small town of about 1,500 people northwest of London. John Shakespeare, William's father, made his living primarily as a tanner and a glover but also traded wool and grain from time to time. John Shakespeare also served (although not at one time) as the town ale taster (inspector of bread and malt), a petty constable, city chamberlain, alderman, and high bailiff (like a mayor), the city's highest public office. Mary Arden, William Shakespeare's mother, brought a long and impressive family lineage to her marriage to John, one that traces itself back to William the Conqueror. In the mid-1570s, John Shakespeare's fortune began to decline mysteriously (some say it was because of his wife's Catholicism, although that claim is unsubstantiated), and it was largely mortgages made on properties Mary brought to the marriage that helped to sustain the family.

Education and Marriage

Shakespeare attended school in Stratford-upon-Avon. Although there are no records to prove his enrollment, critics accept it with considerable certainty. At school, Shakespeare would have studied reading and writing (in English as well as in Latin) and Greek and Roman writers including Horace, Aesop, Ovid, Virgil, Seneca, and Plautus. The extent to which he would have been familiar with the works of such ancient classics is unknown, but studying Shakespeare's plays and long poems suggests he had at least a degree of knowledge about them in their original forms, not merely translations.

In November 1582, at age 18, William Shakespeare married Anne Hathaway, 26. Their first child, Susanna, was born the following May; twins, Hamnet and Judith, followed in 1585. Little information is available regarding Shakespeare's life from the time of the twins' birth until 1592 when he received his first public recognition as an upcoming young dramatist and actor in London. We know that at some point he left his family in Stratford, but we know few specifics. Critics hold several theories. One asserts that during the mysterious seven-year period Shakespeare worked as an assistant master of a grammar school. Another popular theory maintains Shakespeare worked as a butcher's apprentice during this time but ran away to London where he was received into the theater. Another theory holds that during the seven-year period, Shakespeare made a living as a deer poacher who was eventually sent away from Stratford as punishment. Other theories contend Shakespeare was a moneylender, a gardener, a sailor, a lawyer, or even a Franciscan. Unfortunately, though, none of these theories is any more likely than another; no one knows with complete certainty what Shakespeare did between 1585 and 1592. All we know for sure is that by 1592 he had arrived in London, leaving his family behind, and had begun what is perhaps the most successful literary career the world has ever known.

Life in London

Before the Great Plague of 1592–1593, in the time when Shakespeare first came to London, the city boasted several acting troupes. In 1558, when Queen Elizabeth I ascended the throne, any gentleman could maintain a troupe of actors. By 1572, it became illegal for any nobleman below the rank of baron to maintain a troupe, although other companies could perform by obtaining a special license, which had many performance restrictions. Although this arrangement severely restricted the number of acting troupes, it extended governmental sanction to the remaining licensed companies.

When the Great Plague of 1592–1593 hit, closing the theaters and decimating the population of England, many acting companies dissolved, while others were forced to amalgamate with other troupes for survival. Two preeminent companies emerged in 1593, and they would rival each other for years. One company, The Lord Admiral's Men, was headed by Edward Alleyn with financial banking from Philip Henslowe. The other dominant troupe, The Lord Chamberlain's Men (the troupe in which Shakespeare was actor, dramatist, and shareholder, later renamed The King's Men when James I took the throne in 1603), was run by the Burbage family.

Acting troupes were organized under a shareholding plan wherein financial risk and profits were divided among those actors who had become part owners of the company by buying shares in it. The troupes, comprised entirely of men and young boys, employed about 25 actors. Roughly fewer than half of a troupe's actors were shareholders and not all owned equal shares, but those considered especially valuable to the company were encouraged to become shareholders since this ensured their continued service and loyalty. To become a shareholder, an actor had to put up a considerable sum of money; when he retired or died, the company paid the actor or his heirs for his share. Non-shareholding adult members of a company, however, were considered hirelings of the shareholders and worked under contracts promising them a weekly wage of about 5–10 shillings, although they were frequently paid less.

Shakespeare became a shareholding member of The Lord Chamberlain's Men in 1599. Scholars estimate that until about 1603 the average payment for a play was £6 (six pounds); by 1613 the price had risen to £10 or £12. In addition to his fee, the playwright was given all the receipts (minus company expenses) at the second performance (but remember, if the show was bad, there may not *be* a second performance). Once these fees were paid, however, the play was considered property of the troupe. Printers often pirated more popular works, and troupes sometimes sold publication rights during times of financial stress. Such publishing practices, combined with the fact playwrights, including Shakespeare, didn't write with the intention of preserving their plays but with the goal of making money, makes it difficult for scholars to pinpoint definitive texts. In Shakespeare's case, only about half of his plays were published during his lifetime.

In fact, it wasn't until 1623, seven years after Shakespeare's death in 1616, that all his plays were assembled into one volume. This collection, referred to as *The First Folio* (because it was printed in folio format, the largest, most expensive, and most prestigious kind of book), included previously published plays as well as plays never before published. Some of the works in *The First Folio* can be traced to the author's original version of the text (including blotted lines and revisions), yet some were recreated from prompt books (annotated versions of the play script that contain detailed directions for the action, settings, etc.) or even the memories of the actors themselves (helping to explain some of the inconsistencies found in different editions of the plays).

Shakespeare's Work

Between the years of 1588 and 1613, Shakespeare wrote 38 plays. His dramatic work is commonly studied in four categories: comedies, histories, tragedies, and romances. In addition, Shakespeare wrote several Ovidian poems, including *Venus and Adonis* (1593) and *The Rape of Lucrece* (1594). Shakespeare is also well known for his sonnet sequence written in the early 1590s, which is composed of 154 interconnected sonnets dealing with issues such as love, fidelity, mortality, and the artist's power and voice.

Although we commonly single out Shakespeare's work as extraordinary and deserving of special attention, at the time of the plays' performances they were typically dismissed as popular entertainment. Whereas Shakespeare's works are studied today as timeless masterpieces, the original audiences knew the plays were good but did not recognize them as exhibiting the apex of the dramatic art form. In fact, Shakespeare, despite all the attention his name has generated since the late eighteenth century, was not the most popular dramatist of his time. Ben Jonson, Shakespeare's contemporary (and Britain's first Poet Laureate), and Christopher Marlowe, a slight predecessor to Shakespeare, were both commonly held in higher esteem than the man whose reputation has since eclipsed both of his competitors.

In fact, Shakespeare's reputation as Britain's premier dramatist did not begin until the late eighteenth century. His sensibility and storytelling captured people's attention, and by the end of the nineteenth century his reputation was solidly established. Today Shakespeare is more widely studied and performed than any other playwright in the Western world, providing a clear testament to the skills and timelessness of the stories told by the Bard.

INTRODUCTION TO THE PLAY

Introduction

A Midsummer Night's Dream was written in a highly creative period in Shakespeare's career, when he was moving away from the shallow plots that characterized his earlier drama and discovering his more mature style. Most critics believe the play was written for and performed at an aristocratic wedding, with Queen Elizabeth I in attendance. Scholars estimate the play was written in 1595 or 1596 (when Shakespeare was 31 or 32 years old), at approximately the same time as *Romeo and Juliet* and *Richard II*. Obvious plot links exist between *A Midsummer Night's Dream* and *Romeo and Juliet*, and critics disagree about which play was written first. Not only do both dramas emphasize the conflict between love and social convention, but the plot of "Pyramus and Thisbe," the play-within-the-play of *A Midsummer Night's Dream*, parallels that of *Romeo and Juliet*. Critics have wondered if *Romeo and Juliet* is a serious reinterpretation of the other play, or just the opposite: Perhaps Shakespeare is mocking his tragic love story through the burlesque of "Pyramus and Thisbe."

Sources and Allusions

Unlike most of Shakespeare's dramas, *A Midsummer Night's Dream* does not have a single written source. The story of "Pyramus and Thisbe" was originally presented in Ovid's *The Metamorphosis*, making it one of many classical and folkloric allusions in the play. Other allusions include Theseus and Hippolyta's wedding, which is described in Chaucer's "Knight's Tale" in *The Canterbury Tales*, while the theme of a daughter who wants to marry the man of her choice despite her father's opposition was common in Roman comedy. The fairies that dance and frolic throughout this play were most likely derived from English folk tradition. On the one hand, these creatures have a sinister side—Puck, for example, is also known as Robin Goodfellow, a common name for the devil—but they can also be viewed as fun-loving nature spirits, aligned with a benevolent Mother Nature. The interaction of this eclectic array of characters—from the classically Greek royalty such as Theseus (derived from Plutarch's tale of "Theseus" in his *Lives of the Noble Grecians and Romans*) to more traditionally Celtic fairies such as Puck—emphasizes Shakespeare's facility in using elements of the old to create something completely new.

Performance History

The first Quarto edition of the play, printed in 1600, announces that it was "sundry times publickely acted, by the Right honourable, the Lord Chamberlaine his seruants." Indeed, this drama has seen "sundry" performances over the past 400 years. Its spectacle and its emphasis on dance and magic and song have led it to be interpreted and performed in a variety of ways. For example, numerous composers have been inspired by Shakespeare's *Dream*. In 1692, Purcell wrote an operatic version, *The Fairy Queen*, although it contains little of Shakespeare's original story line. In 1826, Mendelsohn composed an overture to *A Midsummer Night's Dream*, which is still popular. The play has also seen many famous, and often infamous, interpretations. For example, the 1900 Beerbohm Tree production had live rabbits hopping around the stage, while Peter Brook's 1970 production was presented on a bare stage that looked like a big white box. Most modern productions of the play, including the 1999 film, emphasize its erotic, savage undertones.

Structure of the Play

Showing his usual dexterity in creating coherent dramatic frameworks, Shakespeare here interweaves four separate plots and four groups of characters. Theseus, the Duke of Athens, and Hippolyta, the Queen of the Amazons and Theseus' fiancée, are the first characters introduced. Theseus is a voice of law and reason in the play, as shown by Egeus' entrance into the drama: Egeus needs Theseus to adjudicate a dispute he is having with his daughter, Hermia. The second plot features Hermia and her three friends, Helena, Demetrius, and Lysander. These young lovers stand on the boundaries of the law; like many adolescents, Lysander and Hermia rebel against authority, in this case, by refusing to accept Theseus' laws and, instead, planning to escape from Athenian tyranny. Although the lovers have one foot in the conventional world of Athens, the play forces them to confront their own irrational and erotic sides as they move temporarily into the forest outside of Athens. By the end of the play, though, they return to the safety of Athens, perhaps still remembering some of the poetry and chaos of their night in the forest. This irrational, magical world is the realm of the play's third group of characters: the fairies. Ruled by Titania and Oberon, the enchanted inhabitants of the forest celebrate the erotic, the poetic, and the beautiful. While this world provides an enticing sojourn for the lovers, it is also dangerous. All of the traditional boundaries break down when the lovers are lost in the woods. Finally, the adventures of Quince, Bottom, and the other amateur actors compose the play's fourth plot layer.

Shakespeare dexterously weaves these four worlds together, by having characters wandering in and out of each other's world, by creating echoes and parallels among the different groups. For example, the themes of love and transformation reverberate through all levels of the play, creating coherence and complexity. Coherence is also produced by the play's emphasis on time. The action is associated with two traditional festivals—Midsummer Eve and May Day—both allied with magic, mayhem, and merriment. To emphasize further the connections between the different groups, many modern directors of the play cast the same actor for the roles of Theseus and Oberon, and for those of Hippolyta and Titania.

Theme

While the play rejoices in the magical power of love to transform our lives, it also reminds us of love's excesses and foolishness. More ominously, it tells of the violence often perpetrated in the name of lust: Mythological references to the tales of Philomela and Perogina, for example, remind us that desire results not only in happy, consensual union, but also in rape. In addition to love's combat with violence, the play shows passion's conflict with reason. For example, Egeus' rigid, patriarchal view of the world clashes with his daughter's notion of love and freedom. Another important theme is the duality between fantasy and reality. Indeed, the play highlights the imagination and its inventions: dreams, illusions, and poetry.

One of the central quotes in the play is Theseus' statement that lovers, madmen, and poets share the same propensity to fantasize (V.1, 7–8). Shakespeare is concerned with the relationship between imagination and reality and with the way our emotions alter our perceptions. Early in the play, for example, Egeus accuses Lysander of bewitching Hermia with love charms and intriguing songs (I.1, 27–32), but the perceptive reader knows this is simply Egeus creating a fantastic excuse to justify his cruel treatment of his daughter. Similarly, Helena recognizes love's blindness and fickleness when she argues that strong emotions such as love can make the vile beautiful (I.1, 232–236)—our perceptions are too often skewed by capricious emotion.

Besides weaving together various themes, the play is also intriguing as a spectacle of dance, music, and costume. Numerous critics have noted the important role of dance in this drama, suggesting that the rhythm of the play's poetry and the movement of the characters in and out of scenes have an underlying dance rhythm.

The Elizabethan Theater

Attending the theater in Shakespeare's time was quite unlike attending a professional performance today. First, the theaters were of two distinct kinds: public and private. The government closely regulated both, but particularly the public theaters. Public theaters such as the one in which Shakespeare made his livelihood were fairly large open-air structures, able to hold about 3,000 people.

In order to compete with rival theaters, as well as the popular pastimes of bullbaiting and bearbaiting, acting troupes changed their show bills often, generally daily. They introduced new plays regularly, helping partially explain why about 2,000 plays were written by more than 250 dramatists between 1590 and the closing of the theaters in 1642. Public performances generally started in the mid-afternoon so spectators could return home by nightfall.

Because of weather, plague, Puritan opposition, and religious observances, theaters often advertised on a day-to-day basis (unlike today when we know in advance the dates a show will run). One of the most memorable advertising techniques troupes employed involved running a specific flag atop the theater to signal a performance that day (a black flag for a tragedy, a red flag for a history, and white flag for a comedy). Scholars estimate that during the first part of the seventeenth century, performances in public theaters took place about 214 days (about 7 months) each year.

Although we commonly associate elaborate lighting and scenery with producing plays, in the public playhouses of Elizabethan England, the only lighting came from natural sources. All action took place in front of a general three-tiered façade, eliminating the need for elaborate sets. Public theaters varied in shape (circular, octagonal, square), yet their purpose was the same: to surround a playing area in such a way as to accommodate a large number of paying spectators. Most theaters had tree-roofed galleries for spectators, one above the other, surrounding the yard. Each theater was also made up of three distinct seating areas, each increasingly more expensive: the pit (standing room only, used primarily by the lower classes), the public gallery (bench seats for the middle classes), and the box seats (appropriate for the Puritan aristocracy).

The private theaters of Shakespeare's day offered a definite alternative to the more common public playhouse. These venues were open to the public, but special considerations made it unusual for commoners to attend. First, the private playhouses accommodated only about 300 spectators. In addition, they provided actual seats for patrons, helping to justify a considerably higher admission than the public theaters. Unlike the open-air theaters, private theaters were roofed and lit by candles, allowing for evening performances (a time when most commoners needed to be doing chores around their own homes). During performances, too, the private theaters would often separate the acts with musical interludes rather than performing the entire play without any intermissions, as they did in the public theaters.

A Brief Synopsis

A Midsummer Night's Dream opens with Theseus and Hippolyta planning their wedding, which takes place in four days. Theseus is upset because time is moving so slowly, but Hippolyta assures him the four days will quickly pass. Their relationship has not always been so loving. Theseus won Hippolyta during a battle.

While they discuss their relationship, Egeus enters with his daughter, Hermia, and her two suitors, Lysander and Demetrius. Hermia is in love with Lysander, but her father wants her to marry Demetrius. Lysander argues that he is as good of a match as Demetrius, but Egeus won't listen. Instead, he declares that if Hermia won't marry Demetrius, she will die: This is the law of Athens and his right as her father. Theseus agrees that Hermia should obey her father but offers her a third option: spending her life in a nunnery. Hermia has until the day of Theseus and Hippolyta's wedding to decide upon her fate.

Upset by Theseus' decree, Lysander comes up with a plan. He and Hermia can escape from Athens and its unjust laws by running away to his widowed aunt's house. Here he and Hermia can marry and live in peace. As they discuss their plans, Helena enters. She is in love with Demetrius and wonders how Hermia managed to capture his heart. Hermia insists she hates Demetrius. She and Lysander then tell Helena about their plan to leave Athens. In a last effort to gain Demetrius' love, Helena decides to tell him of this plot, but she doesn't receive even a "thank you" from her cold-hearted lover.

From the Duke's palace, the scene switches to the cottage of Peter Quince, a carpenter who directs a group of amateur actors in his free time. He has chosen the play "Pyramus and Thisbe" to perform for Theseus' wedding and is in the process of casting roles. Nick Bottom, the weaver, is given the leading role of Pyramus, while Francis Flute, the bellows-mender, wins the female lead, Thisbe. The remainder of the roles are assigned, and the group plans to meet the following night at the Duke's oak for a rehearsal—the same woods where Hermia and Lysander plan to meet on their flight from Athens.

The action of the play now shifts to this fairy-enchanted woods, where Puck, Oberon's joker, speaks with one of Titania's fairies. The fairy recognizes Puck as the troublemaker, Robin Goodfellow. They also discuss the argument between Titania and Oberon; Oberon is angry with Titania because she refuses to give him the Indian boy she is raising. While Puck and the fairy talk, Titania and Oberon enter from opposite ends of the stage. After criticizing each other's infidelities— Titania was supposedly in love with Theseus and Oberon with Hippolyta, among others—Titania reminds Oberon that their argument has led to chaos in the natural world. Oberon says this disaster will end if she relinquishes the Indian boy, but Titania refuses. Oberon hatches a sneaky plan to get the boy back. He sends Puck out to find a plant called love-in-idleness, the juice of which makes any person dote on the next creature he or she sees.

While Puck is out looking for this magical flower, Demetrius and Helena wander past Oberon. As usual, Demetrius insists Helena stop following him; he even vows to harm her if she doesn't leave him alone. Taking pity on Helena, Oberon instructs Puck to put some love juice in Demetrius' eyes at a moment when Helena will be the first person he sees upon waking.

Titania and her fairies are the next to enter the stage, with Oberon secretly following. When Titania falls asleep, Oberon squeezes the love juice in her eyes, hoping a wild beast will be the first creature she sees upon waking. In the meantime, Hermia and Lysander wander near Titania's bower. Lost in the woods, they decide to stop and rest until morning. Puck sees Lysander asleep and assumes he is the nasty Athenian Oberon told him about. He puts the love juice in Lysander's eyes.

Still in pursuit of Demetrius, Helena wanders past and notices the sleeping Lysander. She awakens him, and he immediately falls in love with her. Cautious and heartbroken, Helena assumes Lysander is teasing her, so she runs away. Lysander follows. Hermia awakens, calling out for Lysander's help, because she has just had a nightmare in which a snake ate her heart. She dashes into the woods in search of Lysander.

Quince, Bottom, and the other actors are the next characters to meander near Titania's bower. As they rehearse "Pyramus and Thisbe," Puck secretly listens, appalled by their awful acting. Deciding Bottom is the worst in the bunch, Puck gives him an ass-head. When Bottom saunters out of the woods to deliver his lines, the other actors fly from him in fear. Bottom is unaware of the transformation and walks unworriedly through the woods. Singing as he passes her bower, Bottom awakens Titania who immediately falls in love with him.

Puck explains all of these events to Oberon, who is pleased with the way his plan has turned out. Indeed, everything seems perfect, until Demetrius and Hermia walk past, Hermia believing Demetrius has harmed Lysander, who has mysteriously disappeared. Oberon realizes that Puck has anointed the wrong Athenian with the love juice. Angry with this mistake, Oberon sends Puck in search of Helena, vowing to charm Demetrius' eyes when she appears. Now both Lysander and Demetrius are in love with Helena, adding much to Puck's amusement at the foolishness of mortals. Helena still believes they are teasing her. When Hermia honestly, and confusedly, says she knows nothing about the sudden switch in Lysander's feelings, Helena believes she is simply playing dumb: In her opinion, her three friends are laughing at her.

Before a serious fight breaks out between Demetrius and Lysander, Oberon has Puck create a fog that will keep the lovers from finding one another. While they're sleeping, Puck reverses the spell on Lysander. He also casts a spell so none of the lovers will remember what has happened in the woods. In the meantime, Oberon returns to Titania's bower in search of the Indian boy. Titania willingly releases him because she only has eyes for Bottom. Oberon's plan is now complete, and he is disgusted to see his queen in love with an ass, so he releases her from the spell.

Titania awakens and tells Oberon about her strange dream of being in love with an ass. Oberon has Puck remove the ass-head from Bottom. Now that Oberon has won the Indian boy from Titania, he is willing to forget their argument, and the two, reunited, dance off together so they can bless Theseus' marriage.

Morning has arrived and Theseus, Hippolyta, and Egeus are walking through the woods. Theseus suddenly spies the sleeping lovers and imagines they woke early to observe the rite of May. When the lovers are awakened, Demetrius confesses that he now loves Helena. Theseus decides the other lovers should be married along with him and Hippolyta. As they return to the palace, the scene shifts to Bottom. Just awakening from his dream, Bottom declares he'll have Quince write a ballad about it, called "Bottom's Dream," because it has no bottom.

Quince and the other actors haven't forgotten their missing friend, Bottom. They worry "Pyramus and Thisbe" won't be able to go on without him, which saddens them because Theseus is known for his generosity, and they might have been rewarded with a lifelong pension for their performance. As they lament this lost opportunity, Bottom suddenly returns. His friends want to hear his story, but Bottom tells them there isn't time for that: They must prepare for the play.

In the final scene, the play has come full circle, and all of the cast returns to the palace where Theseus and Hippolyta discuss the strange tale the lovers have told them about the events of the previous evening. The joyous lovers enter, and Theseus decides it is time to plan the festivities for the evening. Of all the possible performances, the play "Pyramus and Thisbe" turns out to be the most promising. Theseus is intrigued by the paradoxical summary of the play, which suggests it is both merry and tragical, tedious and brief. The players finally present their play. Hippolyta is disgusted by their pathetic acting, but Theseus argues that even the best actors create only a brief illusion; the worst must be assisted by an imaginative audience. The play ends with Puck's final speech, in which he apologizes for the weakness of the performance and promises that the next production will be better.

List of Characters

Theseus Duke of Athens, who is marrying Hippolyta as the play begins. He decrees that Hermia must marry Demetrius or be sentenced either to death or to life in a convent. At the end of the play, he insists that all of the lovers marry along with him and Hipplolyta and provides a humorous commentary to accompany the performance of "Pyramus and Thisbe."

Hippolyta Queen of the Amazons, she is betrothed to Theseus. These two were once enemies, and Theseus won her in battle. In this play, she seems to have lost much of her fighting spirit, though she does not hesitate to voice her opinion, for example, following Theseus' choice of the play "Pyramus and Thisbe."

Lysander Hermia's beloved. Egeus does not approve of Lysander, though we don't know why. Lysander claims to be Demetrius' equal, and the play supports this claim—the differences between the two lovers are negligible, if not nonexistent—yet Egeus insists Hermia marry Demetrius. Rather than lose his lover in this random way, Lysander plans to escape with her to his widowed aunt's home. During a night in the forest, Lysander is mistakenly doused by Puck with Oberon's love juice, causing him to fall briefly in love with Helena. Realizing the mistake, Oberon makes Puck reverse the spell, so by the end of the play, Lysander and Hermia are once again in love and marry.

Demetrius He is in love with Hermia, and her father's choice of a husband for her. Similar to Lysander in most ways, Demetrius' only distinguishing characteristic is his fickleness in love. He once loved Helena but has cruelly abandoned her before the play begins. Not only does he reject Helena's deep love for him, but he vows to hurt, even rape, her if she doesn't leave him alone. With the help of Oberon's love juice, he relinquishes Hermia and marries Helena at the end of the play. Demetrius is the only character who is permanently affected by Oberon's love juice.

Hermia Although she loves Lysander, her father insists she marry Demetrius or be put to death for disobedience of his wishes. Theseus softens this death sentence, declaring that Hermia choose Demetrius, death, or life in a convent. Rather than accept this dire fate, Hermia agrees to run away with Lysander. During the chaotic night in the woods, Hermia is shocked to see her beloved abandon her and declare his love for Helena. She is unaware of the mischief Oberon's love juice is playing with Lysander's vision. By the play's end, Puck has reversed the spell, and Lysander's true love for Hermia has been restored. Despite her father's continued opposition to their union, the two marry with Theseus' blessing.

Helena She is the cruelly abused lover of Demetrius. Before the play begins, he has abandoned her in favor of Hermia. Helena doesn't understand the reason for his switch in affection, because she is as beautiful as Hermia. Desperate to win him back, Helena tries anything, even betraying Hermia, her best childhood friend, by revealing to the jealous Demetrius Lysander and Hermia's plan to escape Athens. With the help of Oberon's love juice, Demetrius finally falls back in love with Helena, and the two are married at the end of the play.

Oberon The King of the Fairies, Oberon is fighting with Titania when the play begins because he wants custody of an Indian boy she is raising. He hatches a plan to win the boy away from her by placing love juice in her eyes. This juice causes her to fall rashly in love with Bottom. During her magic-induced love affair, Oberon convinces her to relinquish the boy, who Oberon will use as a page. Once he has the boy, Oberon releases Titania from her spell, and the two lovers are reunited. Oberon also sympathizes with Helena and has Puck place love juice in Demetrius' eyes so he falls in love with her. After Puck mistakenly anoints Lysander, Oberon insists Puck fix his mistake so that the true lovers are together by the end of the play. In the final scene, he and Titania bless all of the newlyweds.

Titania Oberon's wife, she is Queen of the Fairies. Because of Titania's argument with Oberon, the entire human and natural world is in chaos. Oberon wants the Indian boy she is protecting, but Titania refuses to give him up because when his mother died in childbirth, she agreed to raise the boy. Following Oberon's application of the love juice to her eyes, Titania falls in love with Bottom, and Oberon takes the Indian boy from her. Once he has the boy, Oberon releases the spell, and he and Titania are reunited.

Puck, or Robin Goodfellow Oberon's jester, Puck is responsible for mistakenly anointing Lysander with the love juice intended for Demetrius. Puck enjoys the comedy that ensues when Lysander and Demetrius are both in love with Helena but follows Oberon's orders to reunite the correct lovers. Puck has the final words of the play, emphasizing that the entire play was just a dream.

Nick Bottom A weaver, Bottom plays Pyramus. He is the most out-going of the group of actors, wishing to play all of the characters in "Pyramus and Thisbe." Puck transforms him into an ass, and Titania falls in love with him. When Puck returns Bottom to his normal self, Bottom can't speak about what happened to him but vows to have Peter Quince write about it in a ballad to be called "Bottom's Dream."

Egeus Hermia's tyrannical father. He capriciously declares that she must marry Demetrius or be put to death for disobedience; according to the law of Athens, daughters must obey their fathers or forfeit their lives. At the end of the play, he is shocked to learn that Lysander and Hermia tried to flee Athens and insists they should be punished. Theseus overrules him, making the lovers marry instead.

Philostrate Theseus' Master of Revels, he arranges the selection of performances for Theseus' wedding. He tries to dissuade the wedding party from choosing "Pyramus and Thisbe" but is overruled by Theseus.

Peter Quince A carpenter and the director of the group of actors who perform "Pyramus and Thisbe," which he has written for the celebration following Theseus and Hippolyta's wedding.

Francis Flute A bellows-mender, Flute plays the role of Thisbe. He is displeased to be given a woman's role because he wants to let his beard grow, but Quince assures him that he can play the part in a mask.

Tom Snout Snout is a tinker and plays the role of Wall in "Pyramus and Thisbe."

Snug A joiner, he plays the lion in "Pyramus and Thisbe."

Robin Starveling A tailor, he represents Moonshine in "Pyramus and Thisbe."

Peaseblossom, Cobweb, Moth, Mustardseed Titania's fairies.

Character Map

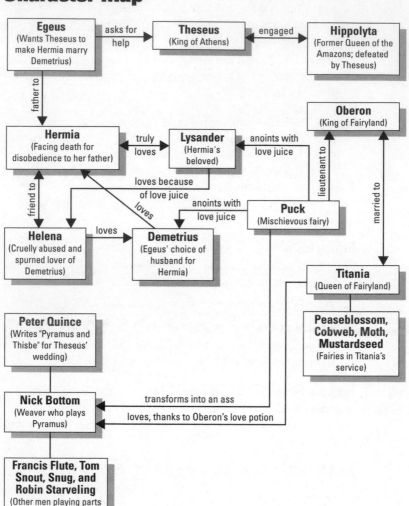

Egeus (Wants Theseus to make Hermia marry Demetrius) — asks for help → **Theseus** (King of Athens) — engaged → **Hippolyta** (Former Queen of the Amazons; defeated by Theseus)

Egeus — father to → **Hermia** (Facing death for disobedience to her father)

Oberon (King of Fairyland)

Hermia — truly loves → **Lysander** (Hermia's beloved) ← anoints with love juice — Puck

Lysander — loves because of love juice → Helena

Hermia — friend to → **Helena** (Cruelly abused and spurned lover of Demetrius)

Helena — loves → **Demetrius** (Egeus' choice of husband for Hermia)

Demetrius — loves → Helena

Puck — anoints with love juice → Demetrius

Puck (Mischievous fairy) — lieutenant to → Oberon

Oberon — married to → **Titania** (Queen of Fairyland)

Peter Quince (Writes "Pyramus and Thisbe" for Theseus' wedding)

Titania (Queen of Fairyland)

Peaseblossom, Cobweb, Moth, Mustardseed (Fairies in Titania's service)

Nick Bottom (Weaver who plays Pyramus) — transforms into an ass; loves, thanks to Oberon's love potion

Francis Flute, Tom Snout, Snug, and Robin Starveling (Other men playing parts in "Pyramus and Thisbe")

CRITICAL COMMENTARIES

Act I, Scene 1

Summary

This scene opens in Theseus' palace in Athens. It is four days before his wedding to Hippolyta, the former queen of the Amazons, and Theseus is impatient with how slowly time is moving. Hippolyta assures him that the wedding day will soon arrive.

As Theseus and Hippolyta plan their wedding festivities, Egeus and his daughter, Hermia, arrive on the scene with Lysander and Demetrius. Egeus is angry because his daughter refuses to marry Demetrius, the man of his choice, but is instead in love with Lysander. Egeus accuses Lysander of bewitching his daughter and stealing her love by underhanded means. Agreeing with Egeus, Theseus declares that it is a daughter's duty to obey her father. Hermia demands to know the worst punishment she will receive for disobedience. Death or spending her life in a nunnery comprise Hermia's choices. Lysander joins the argument, arguing that he is Demetrius' equal in everything and is, indeed, more constant in his affection than Demetrius, who was recently in love with Helena. These proceedings upset Hippolyta, because the prospect of Hermia's death upsets her plans for a happy, festive wedding day.

Finally, everyone except Lysander and Hermia leave the stage. Lysander reminds Hermia that the course of true love has never run smoothly, so they must view their difficulties as typical for lovers. He has a plan for eluding Athenian law: The two lovers will run away from Athens and live with his childless widow aunt to whom he has always been a surrogate son. Living with her, they will be outside of Athenian jurisdiction so that Hermia can avoid Theseus' death sentence and can marry. Having few other options, Hermia is enthusiastic about Lysander's idea and declares her undying love for him.

Just as the lovers have completed their plan for escape, Helena enters the scene. What charms does Hermia possess, Helena wonders, that have so completely captivated Demetrius? Hermia swears that she has no interest in Demetrius, that he actually seems to thrive on her hatred of him. Hermia and Lysander confess their intention of fleeing Athens, and Helena decides to tell Demetrius about it in a final attempt to win his love.

Commentary

Theme

Set in ancient Athens, the play is associated with the gods and goddesses of the Greek pantheon, mythical creatures who often manifested themselves to humans in strange, sometimes terrifying, and often magical ways. Most literary critics believe the play was written to be performed at a private wedding, so while it has a satiric edge, commenting on the difficulties of love, it is also a joyful, festive play, filled with dancing and singing, fairies and enchantment. Drenched in moonlight and filled with dreamers, this play is meant to mesmerize its audience. This scene, for example, opens with Theseus and Hippolyta planning the festivities for their upcoming wedding. Love itself is associated with fantasy and magic, according to Helena. She says thoughts, dreams, sighs, wishes, and tears are all love's minions. Both love's happy and sad aspects are present is this opening scene, which establishes all of the major themes and topics of the drama, including the emphasis on magic and mystical transformations, the often difficult course of true love, and the conflict between imagination and reason.

As its title suggests, this is a play about dreams, and their often illogical, magical, and sensual character. Midsummer's Night is a time of craziness, of mirth and magic. This magic is enacted in the play through the concept of transformation, both personal and general: Helena would like to be "translated" into Hermia, but, more generally, she claims that love transforms everything it looks upon. While Midsummer is the primary setting of the play, references to May Day also abound. For example, Helena and Hermia are supposedly doing "observance of a morn in May" (167). Pagan rituals of May have generally celebrated sexuality and fertility, and this play does not take a Puritanical stance on either subject: The love in this dream is overtly sensual, linked to the songs, dances, and physical pleasures introduced by the fairies. Together these two framing ritual times provide a tone for the play: love and sexuality within a realm of crazy, magical fantasy.

Literary Device

The thematic emphasis on transformation and magic is intensified by the key images of the play, in particular, the recurring references to the moon. Like the moon, which constantly metamorphoses, shedding its old self for something new, the lovers will go through several phases before returning, refreshed and slightly altered, to themselves in Act V. Cyclical, constantly transforming itself in the night sky, the moon is an apt image for the dreamy, moonlit scenes of the play in which characters are constantly transformed. In her three phases—the new, virginal moon of the goddess Diana; the full, pregnant moon of the goddess Luna; and the dark, aging moon of Hecate—the moon is linked with all of the various moods of the play.

In line 3, Theseus connects his wedding to the changes in the moon by assuring Hippolyta that their marriage will occur in four happy days, with the arrival of a new moon. Here Theseus characterizes the moon as a "step-dame" keeping her heir waiting for her death so that he can claim his inheritance. Theseus wants the moon to hurry to her death so he can begin enjoying his "inheritance": marriage to Hippolyta. Hippolyta also associates the moon with love and marriage, declaring it will be "like to a silver bow/ New bent in heaven" (9–10) on the day of their wedding. From stepmother, the moon is transformed in the course of a few lines into the image of fruitful union contained in the "silver bow," an implicit reference to Cupid's arrow, which draws men and women together. Later in the scene, the moon transforms once again, moving into her role as Diana, the chaste goddess of the hunt. Theseus vows that if Hermia does not marry Demetrius as her father wishes, she will live a barren life, "[c]hanting faint hymns to the cold fruitless moon" (73). Theseus says Hermia has until the next new moon to make her decision, so the new moon becomes both a symbol of his happy union with Hippolyta and of Hermia's potential withered life as a nun (or even a corpse), if she does not comply with her father's whim.

Most of Shakespeare's images have similarly multiple layers of significance: Their relevance changes with their context, so no symbol maps simplistically onto a single meaning (in this play, for example, notice also the transformations in the relevance of Cupid and his arrow—sometimes he is a merry matchmaker, while other times he blindly draws people unhappily together). By the end of the scene, the moon presents herself into another of her many names: Phoebe, the queen of moonlit forests. In this role, her "silver visage" will both light and conceal the flight of Lysander and Hermia from Athens, leading them to a happy future beyond the severe authority of Theseus and Egeus. As the play progresses, the moon will continue her transformations, accompanying all of the characters through their magical sojourns.

Love is the primary concern of the play, which begins as Theseus and Hippolyta lament the four long days of waiting before their marriage. But the picture painted of love is not necessarily romantic or simplistic; instead, the play charts the heartaches and the arbitrariness of desire along with its depth, its sighs and tears along with its dreams and wishes. As Lysander tells Hermia, the course of true love never did run true. Often swift, short, and brief, love is besieged by class differences, by age differences, by war, by death, and by sickness. Helena's love is plagued by a different demon: indifference. The more ardently she loves Demetrius, the more thoroughly he hates her. And there seems to be no reason for his disdain: She is as beautiful as Hermia, his new love, as wealthy, as similar to Hermia as "double cherries" on a single stem. Helena's meditations reveal love as arbitrary and, in fact, blind: The childish, blindfolded Cupid, a constantly repeated image in this dream, playfully transforms the vile into something pure and dignified.

Even when love is mutual, it is often hampered by family disapproval. For Lysander and Hermia, love is problematic because of her father's desire for her to marry Demetrius. The law is on his side. All of the relationships in the play, but this one in particular, emphasize the conflict of love and imagination with reason and law. The "ancient privilege of Athens" allows Egeus to "dispose" of his daughter as he wishes: She is his property, so he can "estate" her to anyone.

As is obvious in his choice of words, Egeus views his daughter as little more than an object that he feels he can command as he sees fit. His words also show the violence that often undergirds law or reason: This contrast shows a discord within the seeming concord of love (to paraphrase a saying of Theseus' in Act V). For example, Theseus, the voice of reason and law, wooed Hippolyta with a sword and won her love by "doing her injuries." Although Hippolyta seems subdued, even passive, in the play, the violence that led to their love is a constant presence. This dream of love is not the saccharine view we often see on prime-time television; instead, the play returns us to our animal natures, displaying the primitive, even bestial side of human desire.

While Egeus' willingness to condemn Hermia to death if she refuses to marry Demetrius is astonishing, the arbitrariness of his choice of a son-in-law is even more problematic. Lysander points out that he is as rich, as good-looking, and as successful as Demetrius. In addition, his love of Hermia is true, while Demetrius' love is more fickle, having recently been cruelly transferred to Hermia from his previous lover, Helena.

Theseus' judgement on Hermia isn't as harsh as her father's—marry Demetrius, spend her life in a nunnery or die—yet she has little opportunity for happiness. Notice the military imagery used in the exchange between Theseus and Hermia: For example, Hermia needs to "arm" herself against her father's wishes. She needs to fit her "fancies" to her father's "will" (118), suggesting that Hermia's love and imagination need to be combated by her father's authority or will; otherwise, the law of Athens will sacrifice her on the pyre of reason. Yet, as noted earlier, her father's choice of Demetrius seems as fanciful and arbitrary as Hermia's choice of Lysander. Fortunately, Theseus is less willing than Egeus is to condemn Hermia to death or to celibacy.

In this play, which celebrates love, magic, and sexuality, the choice of a single life is, perhaps, worse than death. Although this play presents the difficulties of love and, in particular, of women's lack of choice in marriage (shown especially strongly through the character of Hippolyta, who appears to have lost all of her spirit following her defeat by Theseus), its goal is to celebrate love and sex; it prefers passion over pedagogy, relationship over celibacy, and life over death.

Glossary

stepdame (5) stepmother.

dowager (5) an elderly woman of wealth and dignity.

faining voice (31) desirous voice.

gauds (33) cheap, showy trinkets, playthings.

filch'd (36) to steal, pilfer.

mew'd (71) to confine in or as in a cage; shut up or conceal.

Diana's altar (89) the altar belonging to the virgin goddess of the moon and of hunting: identified with the Greek Artemis.

spotted (110) morally stained.

Beteem (131) grant.

misgraffed (137) ill-matched.

collied (145) blackened, as with coal dust.

Carthage queen (173) Dido; founder and queen of Carthage: in the Aeneid she falls in love with Aeneas and kills herself when he leaves her.

false Trojan (174) Aeneas, son of Anchises and Venus, and hero of Virgil's *Aeneid:* escaping from ruined Troy, Aeneas wanders for years before coming to Latium: he is considered the forefather of the Romans.

lode-stars (183) stars by which one directs one's course.

translated (191) transformed.

Phoebe (209) Artemis as goddess of the moon: identified with the Roman Diana.

waggish (240) playful.

eyne (242) eye.

Act I, Scene 2

Summary

In this scene, the action shifts to the cottage of Peter Quince, the director of a band of amateur actors who are planning a play to perform for Theseus and Hippolyta's wedding. The play enacts the tragic story of Pyramus and Thisbe, two young lovers who die during a clandestine meeting. Quince is in the process of assigning roles to the various players but meets with many objections to his casting efforts.

Nick Bottom, the weaver who is an entertaining but foolish man, usurps Quince's authority as director and claims he would like to play all of the roles in the drama. He is cast as lover Pyramus. Flute, the bellows mender, is assigned the role of the heroine, Thisbe. Not happy to play a female role because he wants to let his beard grow, Flute is pleased to learn that he can wear a mask for the performance so he won't need to shave. Snug, the joiner, is cast in the role of the lion.

Bottom wants to appropriate this role (as he wanted to appropriate the others), claiming his roar could make the ladies shriek. His statement makes the players nervous. They worry that if the lion is too authentic, the women in the audience will be frightened, literally, to death: They fear that Theseus might have them hanged for scaring the ladies. Bottom agrees to temper his roar, making it gentle as a "sucking dove," but Quince flatters him by insisting that Snug must keep the part of the lion because only Bottom can play the leading role of Pyramus. When the casting is finally finished, Quince sends the players off to learn their lines and tells them to meet for a rehearsal the following evening at the Duke's oak.

Commentary

Theme

The tone and atmosphere of the play change in this scene along with the setting. From the palace of the Duke, we move to the home of Quince, a working-class man. With the entry of the players into the action, Shakespeare introduces the notion of class difference and provides a reflection on the position and character of actors within society.

While this scene seems to provide a complete contrast with the previous scene, there is also some continuity in the action. For example, the play-within-the-play, "Pyramus and Thisbe," presents a story of misguided lovers, continuing the overall drama's obsession with love and, in particular, with the often crooked course of love, which, as Lysander proclaimed in the previous scene, never runs true.

"Pyramus and Thisbe" also provides thematic continuity with other plays within Shakespeare's *ouevre*, in particular with *Romeo and Juliet*, which most critics believe was written shortly before *Dream*. Both recount the tragic fate of true lovers who kill themselves finding their mistresses seemingly dead. Pyramus kills himself when he thinks that Thisbe has been devoured by a lion, just as Romeo stabs himself after finding Juliet seemingly dead in the tomb of the Capulets. This tragic theme does not necessarily seem appropriate in a play that was supposedly written to be performed at a wedding celebration, but the tragedy here is tempered with mirth. The inept attempts of the players transform Pyramus and Thisbe's sad story into a burlesque.

Although *Dream* obviously makes reference to Pyramus and Thisbe and to numerous mythological stories, its plot is not based, like most of Shakespeare's other plays, on one particular primary source. The play makes many general allusions to Chaucer's *Knight's Tale* and to Spencer's *The Faerie Queen*, and Oberon's name and the stories of Theseus and Hippolyta are adapted from Greek mythology. Because the play was most likely written for a wedding celebration, that occasion provided all the authority the play required.

Bottom is often considered to be one of the most exuberant characters in Shakespeare's work. Although his egotism and lack of self-reflection have been criticized, Bottom's vitality makes him a favorite with theater-goers. In this scene, for example, his willingness to play any and all roles in the play shows his fearlessness, his eagerness to become a leader. Bottom's attractiveness lies not only in his often asinine personality, but in his clumsy command of language.

Bottom's language is often paradoxical, as when he claims he would speak in a "monstrous little voice" if he had the role of Thisbe: Can a voice be simultaneously monstrous and little? Somehow the audience believes that Bottom could achieve such a feat. In addition to paradox, Bottom's speech is also full of malapropisms (incorrect usages of words): For example, he claims that he will "aggravate" his voice when he plays the role of the gentle lion when he really means "mitigate" (or lower)

it. Similarly, he encourages the other players to rehearse "most obscenely," when he probably wants their practice to be "seemly." Yet critics have noted that his incorrect usage is, at bottom, correct. To some, the misguided attempts of these lower-class actors could be viewed as "obscene" rather than seemly, and in his role as lion, Bottom would most likely be aggravating!

The title of the play-within-the-play contains a similar comic element. Quince has titled his drama "The most lamentable comedy, and most cruel death of Pyramus and Thisbe," quite accurately representing the paradoxical nature of their unique performance of this drama. Just as love is often a blend of tears, sighs, and joy, Quince's brand of comedy (and Shakespeare's as well) complexly blends the violent with the playful, almost absurd.

Shakespeare's goal in creating this play-within-the-play was to add a comic element to the action. But why does he present these actors as fools? Perhaps to highlight the ineptitude of many of the other acting companies of his day, while emphasizing the superiority of his own company; presumably, they were not as ridiculous as Quince and his merry band of actors. Perhaps Shakespeare used this technique to accentuate the theatrical elements of his own drama, forcing the audience to think more carefully about the relationship between drama and reality. The players are humorous partly because of their belief in the audience's gullibility: Because they worry that their acting will be too close to reality, they must temper their lion's roar or they will be hanged for frightening their audience, making them think that a death has actually occurred on the stage. By playing their parts too well, the actors fear they will break the walls separating reality from fantasy, which could result in their very real deaths. Of course, to the savvy audience, this seems like a joke—we can all distinguish dream from waking life, theater from reality, can't we?

Theme

Yet these amateur actors also make us reflect upon this very question. Dreams work on many levels within Shakespeare's works. This play is itself a dream, a magical journey in which the characters become involved in a fairy world that impacts their real lives—Oberon's potion makes Demetrius fall in love with Helena, and this change in his personality is never altered. Shakespeare's drama is meant to enact a similar magic on its seemingly savvy audience; perhaps we, like Bottom's ideal audience, will be transported into the dream despite ourselves? Perhaps we have also been captivated by the dream of Shakespeare as literary and cultural icon? These questions emphasize the importance of reflecting on the boundary between drama and fantasy as something that is never stable, but always shifting. If Shakespeare's plays have a real impact on our lives, are they real or fantasy? How does our story of Shakespeare, or of literature in general, alter our understanding of the nature of dreams? It does not seem insignificant that Bottom is a weaver by trade—weaving has traditionally been a metaphor for casting a spell, and dreams are often viewed as webs that entrap the unwary dreamer.

A final, less philosophical function of the play-within-the-play is that it verifies many of our cultural stereotypes of actors. For example, Bottom is the star who always wants to steal the show. He is also an actor who seems more interested in his costume than his role; notice how much more time he spends worrying about the minor details of the performance—which color beard he should wear, for example—than he spends worrying about his lines. Quince, on the other hand, is the diplomatic director who carefully manipulates/orchestrates his cast to make them conform to his vision of the play. He assures Flute that he can play the role of Thisbe in a mask, so that his, most-likely imaginary, beard can grow, and he convinces Bottom that he's the only actor with sufficient skill to play the role of Pyramus.

Glossary

scrip (3) script.

Marry (9) [Archaic] interjection used to express surprise, anger, etc., or, sometimes, merely to provide emphasis; here, a mild oath, referring to the Virgin Mary.

humours (21) inclinations.

Ercles (22) Hercules.

Phibbus' car (27) the chariot of Phoebus (Apollo as god of the sun).

That's all one (39) It makes no difference.

Act II, Scene 1

Summary

This scene transports its viewers from Athens into the woods outside of the city, the dwelling place of Oberon, Titania, and their band of fairies. The scene begins with a conversation between Oberon's mischievous elf Robin Goodfellow, also known as Puck, and one of Titania's attendants. Puck warns her to keep Titania away from this part of the woods because Oberon will be reveling here, and if the two meet there will certainly be a serious quarrel. Oberon is angry with Titania because she refuses to give him a sweet Indian boy upon whom she dotes. Titania's attendant suddenly recognizes Puck, accusing him of being the hobgoblin who is blamed for roguish acts in the village, such as frightening young women or misleading night travelers. Puck admits that he is this "merry wanderer of the night."

Suddenly Oberon and Titania enter the scene from opposite directions. Their bickering begins. Each accuses the other of having had affairs, and Titania says Oberon's persecution of her has caused the current chaos in the world: The rivers are flooding, the corn is rotting, and people are plagued by "rheumatic" diseases. Oberon blames Titania; if she would simply relinquish the Indian boy, peace would be restored. Titania refuses to let the boy go because his mother was a close friend of hers, and when she died in childbirth, Titania agreed to raise her son.

Hatching a plan to win the Indian boy, Oberon sends Puck in search of a flower called love-in-idleness. When the juice of this magical flower is poured on sleepers' eyelids, it makes them dote crazily on the first live creature they see upon awakening. In this way, Oberon plans to make Titania fall in love with some wild beast; he won't release her from this unpleasant spell until she gives him the Indian boy.

After Puck has left in search of the powerful flower, Oberon sits scheming. Demetrius and Helena unknowingly stumble into his bower, but he is invisible to them. Helena actively pursues her beloved, but Demetrius vows to hurt her if she doesn't leave him alone. After they have left, Puck returns. Taking pity on Helena, Oberon tells Puck to anoint the eyes of the Athenian man (Demetrius) so that he will fall in love with this jilted woman. Puck promises to fulfill Oberon's order, though Puck hasn't seen Demetrius, so he doesn't know which Athenian Oberon is talking about.

Commentary

From the world of Athens, ruled by the rational Theseus, the play transports us to the fairy-infested woods, dominated by the magical Oberon and Titania. Despite the differences in atmosphere of the various scenes, the theme remains the same: love in all of its variations. In the opening conversation between Puck and Titania's fairy, they discuss the fight between the rulers of the fairy world, providing another example of a love that is not going smoothly. Titania has foresworn the "bed and company" of Oberon (62), and their conversation focuses on the infidelities committed by each: Not only was Oberon once in love with the "bouncing Amazon," Hippolyta, but Titania was supposedly enamoured of Theseus. While the previous scenes presented couples newly embarked on the road of love, the conversation between Oberon and Titania shows the difficulties of a couple that has been together for a long time. Without their guiding love, the entire land has been ravaged by floods, rotting crops, and numerous rheumatic diseases. Notice how the fairy world is directly connected with the cycles of the moon: as "governess of the floods" (103), the moon, which is pale in anger because of Titania and Oberon's argument, has indirectly caused numerous human illnesses.

The scene not only reiterates the difficulties of male-female love but emphasizes the deep love that often exists between two friends. A primary source of the argument between Oberon and Titania is the Indian boy. While Oberon criticizes Titania for stealing the child from the Indian king, Titania's reasons for keeping the child are more personal. Titania was good friends with the boy's mother, one of her priestesses, with whom she would often sit gossiping. In beautifully lyrical language, Titania describes the pregnancy of her friend, which caused her to grow "big-bellied" as gracefully as the sails, filled by the wind of the trading ships that floated in and out of the Indian ports. When her friend died in childbirth, Titania chose to raise her friend's son. The beauty of Titania's language in describing her friend emphasizes the depth of their friendship.

So why is Oberon so fixated on stealing the boy and employing him as henchman (meaning page)? Shakespeare never explains Oberon's reasons. Perhaps Oberon is jealous of the close bond between Titania and the child, a relationship from which Oberon seems firmly excluded, or perhaps he simply wants to assert his male authority over Titania. Literary critics have also suggested that perhaps Oberon is desperate for a male heir, and the child could fulfill that role. In a subtler argument, the critic Harold Bloom has argued that the key dilemma hinges on the relationship of mortals and immortals: Excluding Oberon from the life of this mortal child, one who will learn the magical secrets of the fairies, is an "injury" enacted upon the entire fairy world. As one of the leaders of this community, Oberon has every right to participate in decisions made in determining how this changeling is raised. But we will never know the answer to this question because, Shakespeare tells us, each reader is free to discover the solution that best fits with the details in the rest of the play and with the reader's own preferences.

To win the child back from Titania, Oberon invokes the first real magic in the play, creating a clear link between reality and fantasy. His plan is to steal the Indian boy from Titania after making her fall in love with some unsavory, preferably beastly, character. He will accomplish this task by creating a love potion that will blind Titania, much as Cupid's arrows are reputed to do. The juice works by impairing vision: Oberon says that the love juice will charm Titania's sight, again emphasizing that love is often blind.

Literary Device

The scene in which Oberon discusses his plan to find the plant called love-in-idleness, the key ingredient of this potion, is filled with relevant imagery and allusions. First, Oberon discusses Cupid loosing an arrow upon a "fair vestal, throned by the west" 158). Most critics believe that this fair vestal is Queen Elizabeth, the implicit patroness of this play, which was probably written for a wedding celebration that she attended. Like this "imperial votress," who avoids Cupid's "fiery shaft," Elizabeth never married and supposedly remained a virgin throughout her life. In missing Elizabeth, the arrow instead falls upon the tiny pansy called love-in-idleness, which has become a potent love juice. Forgoing love herself, Elizabeth has unleashed love into the world. This passage also continues the moon imagery of previous scenes: the "chaste," "cold" moon is associated with the goddess Diana and with Elizabeth.

In the final section of this scene, the human world interacts with the fairy realm, as Demetrius and Helena unknowingly infringe upon Oberon's dominion. Helena represents a character completely overwhelmed by love; she has relinquished all self-respect in her pursuit of Demetrius. As she says, the more he beats her, the more she will love him. Groveling before him, she is willing to be used as he uses his dog. Their interaction has a violent edge, as Demetrius vows he will leave her to the mercy of wild beasts or even potentially rape her if she does not leave him alone. Even his harshest statements have no tempering influence on Helena's obsessive affection. This interaction between Demetrius and Helena highlights the often violent subtext of this play, and suggests that strong emotions such as love often feed into other, less desirable but equally strong behaviors, like violence.

Theme

The gender switch in Helena and Demetrius' conversation adds an interesting component to the play's representation of love because it reminds us that men and women are limited by the types of roles they are traditionally allowed when seeking love. Helena invokes male prerogative in pursing Demetrius, reversing many of the myths that abound of men chasing women: She will be Apollo to his Daphne, the griffin to his dove, the tiger to his doe. All of these examples suggest male creatures violating a female, often sexually. Helena seems aware of her odd position in relationship with her beloved. She argues that women aren't allowed to fight for love in the same way men do, so her pursuit of Demetrius makes him hate her, perhaps because it displays an unfeminine aggressiveness.

Of course, Helena is not the only woman in the text who acts on the edge of gender boundaries. As we learned in the opening scene, Hippolyta was once a fighter, the respected leader of the Amazons, a band of warrior women. Like Hippolyta, Theseus' warrior bride, Helena usurped a traditionally male role of dominance and power; like Hippolyta, she needs to be subdued. Although she will probably never be the fighter Hippolyta once was, Helena's attempt to control her own destiny in love causes problems for the male world. Perhaps this is why Helena is rewarded for her faithfulness. Oberon supports her cause by vowing to use the love juice on Demetrius, leaving him fonder of her than she is of him and returning her to a submissive, traditionally feminine position.

Glossary

lob (16) a big, slow, clumsy person.

quern (36) a primitive hand mill, especially for grinding grain.

bootless (37) in vain.

barm (38) the yeast foam that appears on the surface of malt liquors as they ferment.

dewlap (50) a loose fold of skin hanging from the throat of cattle and certain other animals, or a similar loose fold under the chin of a person.

neeze (56) sneeze.

Corin, Phillida (66, 68) conventional names of pastoral lovers.

buskin'd (71) wearing boots reaching to the calf or knee.

Perigouna (78) one of Theseus' lovers.

Aegles (79) the woman for whom Theseus abandoned Ariadne.

Ariadne (80) King Minos' daughter, who gives Theseus the thread by which he finds his way out of the labyrinth after killing the Minotaur.

Antiopa (80) Queen of the Amazons, often identified with Hippolyta, but here they are viewed as separate women.

nine-men's morris (98) pattern cut in the turf when this game was played outside with nine pebbles.

old Hiems (109) the winter god.

childing (112) pregnant.

wonted liveries (113) accustomed attire.

mazed (113) bewildered.

love-in-idleness (116) pansy, heartsease.

wood (192) insane.

adamant (195) lodestone, a hard stone or substance that was supposedly unbreakable.

Apollo (231) the god of music, poetry, prophecy, and medicine, represented as exemplifying manly youth and beauty.

Daphne (231) a nymph who is changed into a laurel tree to escape Apollo's unwanted advances.

hind (232) the female of the red deer.

oxlips (250) a perennial plant of the primrose family.

woodbine (251) a European climbing honeysuckle with fragrant, yellowish-white flowers.

muskroses (252) Mediterranean roses with fragrant, usually white, flowers.

eglantine (252) European rose with hooked spines, sweet-scented leaves, and usually pink flowers.

Act II, Scene 2

Summary

Titania's fairies sing her a soothing lullaby as she prepares for sleep. While she rests, Oberon creeps up, squeezes the potion onto her eyelids and utters a spell to make her awaken when something vile is near.

When Oberon leaves, Lysander and Hermia wander into Titania's bower, but she is invisible to them. The lovers are lost, and Lysander suggests they stop to sleep for the night. Hermia agrees but won't let him sleep too close to her, even though Lysander claims that, because they are engaged, they can sleep innocently side by side. But Hermia insists on separation, so they sleep a short distance apart. After they have fallen asleep, Puck enters, searching for the Athenian whose eyes Oberon wanted him to anoint with the love juice. Seeing Lysander and Hermia lying apart from each other, he mistakes them for Demetrius and Helena and erroneously applies the magical juice to Lysander.

After Puck exits, Demetrius and Helena run into the bower. Helena is in frantic pursuit of her beloved, but he manages to flee his pursuer and sprints into the woods. Depressed and exhausted, Helena stops to rest and notices Lysander asleep on the ground. She wakes him and, thanks to Puck's potion, he immediately falls in love with her. When he claims to have abandoned Hermia, who he now describes as dull and unattractive, Helena assumes he is teasing her so she runs away. Lysander chases after her, and Hermia awakens. She has been dreaming about a fearful snake that ate her heart awake. Frightened that Lysander has disappeared, she, too, rushes into the woods.

Commentary

With its entry into Titania's festive bower, the play fills with singing and dancing. The fairies sing a lullaby for Titania as they perform their duties of keeping all unpleasantness—spotted snakes, spiders, and beetles—away from their queen. Titania's world abounds with beauty, and her songs are filled with references to the natural world, over which she rules. While her fairies work to keep the insects and smaller beasts away, Oberon invokes larger animals into her bower: leopards or boars or bears. Notice that he, in particular, wants the love potion to make her fall in love with something "vile." This detail seems to suggest an element of maliciousness in Oberon's attempts to lure the Indian boy away, perhaps supporting the idea that he is jealous of the boy's relationship with Titania. In fact, his spiteful behavior toward Titania contrasts with his compassion for Helena and the other humans in the play. While he is a benevolent ruler where humans are concerned, his kindness does not necessarily extend to his own kin.

The worlds of the humans and fairies become further linked in this scene, as Puck applies the love potion to Lysander's eyes: The humans are now full participants in the fairies' magical world. Many performances of the play emphasize not only its obsession with love, but its focus on sexuality. Remember that in Act I, Scene 1, Theseus suggested that chastity was a fate almost worse than death, and Act II, Scene 1 listed all of Oberon and Titania's infidelities. Now Lysander and Hermia are spending the night together in the woods as they flee Athens. For them, the question is how close together they can modestly sleep.

Like most young men, Lysander believes that closer is better, arguing for "one bed, two bosoms, and one troth," but Hermia does not want him so near. Although Lysander emphasizes the innocence of his intentions, especially because of their engagement, Hermia believes that separation is necessary in order for them to maintain their virtuousness: For her, an external show of virtue is as important as internal innocence. Lysander accepts her logic, vowing that he will love her until he dies— but love is capricious, as the play soon shows, and such promises of fidelity are often no sooner spoken than they are broken. When Puck sees the two lovers sleeping separately, he does not interpret their distance as a sign of modesty. Instead, he assumes that Lysander is the "lack-love" Demetrius and that Hermia is not sleeping close to him because he's such a lout. For the fairies, modesty does not seem to be a virtue; they believe love should be expressed.

Style & Language

The language used in this scene once again suggests that love is a matter of vision. Puck puts potion on Lysander's eyes in order to "charm" his sight. Helena wishes she could be transformed into Hermia whose eyes are "blessed and attractive" (90) and believes her own ugliness lies in her eyes. How could her own teary eyes be compared with Hermia's, which are as sphery as the stars? When Lysander falls in love with Helena under the spell of the love-in-idleness, he applauds her transparency, which allows him to see into her heart. Similarly, he can see love's stories written in her eyes, which contain "love's richest book" (121). Apparently, love is based entirely upon looks, upon attractiveness, and the source of this attraction resides in the eyes, which, after all, are windows to the soul. The narrative of love is conveyed through the exchange of looks, through vision that reveals the soul. Helena longs for a "sweet look" (126) from Demetrius' eyes, a look that will reveal his attraction for her and that will allow her to see the story of her love for him. This scene also plays with the notion of love at first sight: While *Romeo and Juliet* presents this as a valid form of love, applauding their instant devotion, this play is more suspicious of such seeming love. Lysander's instant love at the sight of Helena seems more a sign of his lack of fidelity than of true love.

Linked to the emphasis on vision is Lysander's resort to logic, which is a form of clear-sightedness. While he had earlier declared his undying love for Hermia with the language of emotion, Lysander now explains his new, fickle preference for Helena in terms of reason, which says that she is "the worthier maid," yet he provides no reasons for this judgment. In fact, the characters of Hermia and Helena seem fairly interchangeable in the play, as are Lysander and Demetrius, so it is difficult for readers to know what might make Helena or Hermia a better choice as a lover. What is the source of his love for Hermia? Shakespeare never says, perhaps because he wants to emphasize love's arbitrary nature. Lysander claims he is now mature and his reason is better developed, allowing him to see Hermia's faults and Helena's strengths, yet the play gives no indication that Lysander has, indeed, changed. Similarly, it provides no detail to support these differences between the two women. Lysander's claims are particularly ludicrous to members of the audience, who know the reason for the change in his mood isn't his new maturity, but Puck's magic.

Literary Device

In this play, magic has the power to transform lovers, and dreams are prophetic of the future. The scene ends with Hermia awakening from a dream in which a crawling serpent ate at her heart, while Lysander watched and smiled. Serpents have numerous negative connotations in Western culture—they are associated with sexuality, with the betrayal in the Garden of Eden, and with Eve's movement from innocence to knowledge. All of these connotations are relevant in this context. Hermia is sleeping in a bower of bliss, but not the innocent paradise of Christian mythology; rather, she is in the more sexually potent bower of Titania and Oberon. While the natural world of the forest is often associated with innocence and the city with experience, this play reverses that dichotomy: Hermia appears to move toward experience following her night in the woods. No longer will she trust Lysander's vows of eternal devotion, after seeing how quickly his love changed following his encounter with Helena. She will soon move from innocent trust in male vows of love to a wary despair over men's unfaithfulness.

Glossary

roundel (1) round dance.

reremice (4) bats.

Philomel (13) the nightingale (Philomela was a princess of Athens raped by Tereseus; the gods change her into a nightingale).

ounce (36) snow leopard.

Pard (37) leopard, or panther.

troth (48) faithfulness; loyalty.

beshrew (60) to curse, usually mildly.

Act III, Scene 1

Summary

Comedy returns to the play in the opening of this scene. Peter Quince and his company are rehearsing their rendition of Pyramus and Thisbe. Bottom has serious reservations about the play: Pyramus kills himself with a sword, and the lion is frightening, both factors that are sure to terrify the women in the audience. The other players agree, wondering if the play should be abandoned, but Bottom has a solution. A prologue needs to be written to explain that Pyramus is only an actor, and the actor playing the lion must show half of his face during his performance and tell the audience his true identity. With these problems successfully solved, Quince mentions two other difficulties with the upcoming performance: It requires moonshine and a wall. After consulting a calendar, they discover that the moon will be shining on the night of the performance, so they can simply leave a window open. The wall is a greater dilemma for these silly men. Finally, Bottom discovers a solution: An actor covered in plaster will play the role of the wall. Everyone agrees, and the rehearsal begins.

Puck eavesdrops on the performance, amused by the way these actors butcher their lines. The egotistical Bottom sits in the bushes, waiting his cue, and Puck can't resist playing a joke on him: He gives Bottom an ass' head. When Bottom enters, declaring his love for Thisbe, the other terrified actors dash into the woods. Unaware of his transformation, Bottom has no idea what has frightened them. As he walks singing through the woods, Titania, with the love juice on her eyes, awakens and falls immediately in love with the beastly Bottom. She appoints four fairies—Peaseblossom, Cobweb, Mote, and Mustardseed—to serve the needs of her new lover.

Commentary

The play's humor continues in this scene through the vehicle of the players. As in Act I, Scene 1, their belief in the audience's gullibility is highlighted. Bottom has found a new objection to the play: Pyramus must kill himself, which will offend the women in the audience. Again, his comments show his belief that the audience will be unable to differentiate reality from fantasy. To combat this problem, Bottom proposes an elaborate Prologue that will explain Pyramus' identity. Similarly, the lion must show half of his face so the audience will know he is a man rather than a beast. Quince brings two other difficulties to the players' attention: how the moonlight and the wall will be presented.

Style & Language

Again the question hinges on the problem of representation: In the players' opinion, the audience possesses a strong imagination, so with the correct costuming, a man can impersonate any object. For example, with some plaster on his clothing, Snout can become a wall; with a lantern, he can "disfigure," according to Quince, moonshine. Quince's malapropism here is comical, yet correct: These players do, indeed, "disfigure," rather than "figure" (the word Quince meant to use) the characters they play. Similarly, Bottom's misuse of words continues to be funny in this scene, partially because, at bottom, they are correct, given the context of these actors' inept performance; for example, he says "defect" rather than "effect" in line 38 or "odious" rather than "odorous" in lines 78–79. In all of these circumstances, Shakespeare assumes an audience intelligent enough to recognize Bottom's misuses but equally capable of seeing the comic correctness in Bottom's mistakes.

The wall between reality and fantasy breaks down as the scene continues. While Bottom presented an ineffective impersonation of Pyramus, he offers a stunning performance of an ass. The players are clearly taken in by Bottom's new guise, sprinting out of the woods to escape what they see as a haunting. Puck's magic is similar to the actors'. In fact, when he first sees them rehearsing, Puck claims that he'll become an actor, if necessary, and says that he can effectively translate himself into numerous other characters: a horse, a hound, a hog, a headless bear, a fire. Puck is the ideal actor, able to personify any role with haunting veracity. Indeed, his art seems to be Shakespeare's ideal for actors—like Puck, they should prey on their audience's imaginations, breaking the walls between imagination and reason, leading us to new worlds, haunting us with visions our rational minds cannot comprehend. Puck is also the ideal director, casting Bottom in the role for which he is most suited: ass. Following his transformation, the asinine Bottom literally portrays what he has always been metaphorically.

Bottom's lack of surprise at his new role adds comic flavor to his interactions with Titania. When she professes her love for him, erroneously calling him an "angel," he is not astonished. Her misrecognition of this ass as an angel, caused by Oberon's powerful love potion, provides a powerful example of the inadequacy of using vision as the basis of love: She claims Bottom's shape has "enthralled" her so much that she fell in love with him on "first view" (134, 136). Although usually foolish, Bottom's response to her hyperbolic protestations of love shows his down-to-earth nature. For example, when Titania declares him both wise and beautiful, Bottom recognizes the error of her statements, affirming that he is neither. But this does not mean he is intimidated by her.

Rather than being surprised or flattered that the Queen of the Fairies has fallen in love with him, Bottom, instead, remarks that she has little reason for loving him, yet adds that "reason and love keep little company together nowadays" (138–139), so her admiration is understandable, if not necessarily natural. In Bottom's opinion, love and reason should become friends. His speech echoes Lysander's in the previous scene. Remember that Lysander believed his newfound love for Helena was based on reason. The characters in this drama are attempting to find a way to understand the workings of love in a rational way, yet their failures emphasize the difficulty of this endeavor. Shakespeare seems to be suggesting that a love potion, even though seemingly crazy, is a better way to explain the mysterious workings of sexual attraction than is common sense: Love and reason will never be friends.

Bottom's interactions with the fairies at the end of the scene are significant because they reemphasize the comical differences between Titania and the ass-headed Bottom. While she speaks in lyrical prose, a beautiful language filled with natural and delicate imagery— dewberries, painted butterflies, and moonbeams bedeck her speech— Bottom's language lacks this lyrical grace. Rather than yearning for the jewels she promises or the bed made of pressed flowers, Bottom straightforwardly identifies the fairies with the tasks their names suggest; he has no interest in the magical, more figurative functions they could perform for him. For example, Mustardseed is simply a spice made to flavor his beef. Bottom's prosaic approach to language appears to annoy the poetic Titania who asks her fairies to tie up Bottom's tongue before bringing him to her bower. Shakespeare has not forgotten the moon in this scene. A "watery" moon shines in Titania's final speech, weeping along with the flowers at any violated chastity.

Glossary

tiring-house (4) attiring house.

Byrlakin (11) by your ladykin (i.e., the Virgin Mary).

disfigure (47) Quince's blunder for "figure."

Ninny/Ninus (80) mythical founder of Ninevah.

ouzel cock (102) male blackbird.

throstle (104) a songbird.

quill (105) the bird's piping song.

gleek (121) jest.

Mote (135) a speck of dust.

gambol (139) frolic.

Peascod (160) the pod of the pea plant.

enforced (171) violated by force.

Act III, Scene 2

Summary

Encountering Oberon in another part of the forest, Puck explains the outcome of his experiments with the love potion. Oberon is pleased to learn that Titania has fallen in love with the monstrous Bottom and that Puck has also fixed the disdainful Athenian. Just after Puck assures him that Demetrius must now love Helena, Demetrius and Hermia enter the scene. Oberon recognizes Demetrius, but Puck realizes this is not the same Athenian he bewitched with the potion. Because her darling Lysander has mysteriously disappeared, Hermia accuses Demetrius of murdering him and hiding the body. Demetrius insists that he didn't kill his enemy, but Hermia refuses to believe him. Giving up the argument in despair, Demetrius sinks to the ground and falls asleep, while Hermia continues her search for the missing Lysander.

Oberon reprimands Puck for anointing the wrong Athenian with the love juice. To correct the situation, Oberon sends Puck in search of Helena and then squeezes the magic potion into the cold-hearted Demetrius' eyes. Lysander and Helena enter the scene, still bickering because Helena thinks he is mocking her. Their voices wake Demetrius, who falls in love with Helena at first sight, compliments of Oberon's potion. Hearing what she believes are Demetrius' phony declarations of love, Helena is furious: Both Lysander and Demetrius are now making fun of her. When Hermia enters, the situation gets even worse.

Not knowing about the potion-induced change in Lysander's feelings for her, Hermia is shocked when he declares he no longer loves her. Of course, Helena thinks that Hermia is also in on the farce and can't believe her closest childhood friend could be so nasty. After the lovers have all fought and fled the scene, Oberon forces Puck to fix the problem before the men kill each other. He advises Puck to create a deep fog in which the lovers will get lost and, finally, fall asleep in exhaustion. When they awake in the morning, the night's crazy events will seem like a dream except that Demetrius will be in love with Helena. Oberon then rushes to Titania's bower to beg for the Indian boy.

Commentary

Shakespeare's parody of love reaches its peak in this scene. Although Hermia claims Lysander's love is truer than the sun onto the day, previous scenes have shown that his love was easily altered with the application of a little love juice. When Oberon criticizes Puck for turning a true love false, rather than a false love true, Puck replies, "one man holding troth, / A million fail, confounding oath on oath" (92–93), suggesting only one man in a million is actually able to be true to his vows of love; all others break oath on oath, including the seemingly true Lysander. The comedy of the situation appeals to Puck, who muses on what fools "mortals be."

Style & Language

In declaring his love for Helena, Demetrius focuses first on her eyes, which he believes are clearer than crystal. Her lips are luscious fruit, like ripe and tempting cherries, but, more interestingly, he emphasizes her "whiteness." She is a pure white, like the snow on top of some high summit; indeed, in his eyes she is a "princess of pure white." The emphasis on white links her with purity, with innocence, with the dazzling, blinding light of a snow-covered field. But it also has a racial overtone. As whiteness becomes associated with purity, darkness becomes linked with its opposite, with evil. This creates a hierarchical dichotomy in which whiteness is prized and darkness is denigrated. As a result, dark-skinned people are also maligned, as happens here with Hermia. Lysander critiques her by labeling her an "Ethiope" and a "tawny Tartar" and implying that her darkness makes her somehow inferior to Helena.

Not surprisingly, Helena is angered by what she views as her friends toying with her, so she adds to the criticism by commenting on Hermia's stature. Indeed, height seems to play a role in love, and Hemia seems to believe that Lysander loves Helena simply because she is the taller of the two women. This exchange emphasizes the arbitrariness of the factors that create or repel love: eye color, hair color, height.

Like Helena earlier in the play, Hermia is here pushed beyond the limits of "maiden's patience" (66) when dealing with love, women forget the gender limits that have been imposed upon them, perhaps because they are judged by such seemingly ridiculous standards. Retaliating against suggestions that she is small, even dwarfish, Hermia calls Helena a "painted maypole." This comment implies a double critique: not only is Helena as skinny as a pole, but she is "painted," suggesting she is sexually knowledgeable. The fight that ensues between the two women puts them both beyond the limits of supposedly feminine gentleness. Helena further critiques Hermia by calling her "keen," "shrewd," and a "vixen." A short shrew, Hermia is not the ideal woman.

Literary Device

In calling Demetrius a serpent, an adder, Hermia creates continuity with Act II, Scene 2, in which she dreamed that a serpent ate her heart out. But in this instance, Hermia mistakes the snake; Demetrius has not killed Lysander, but her heart will soon be pierced with an even greater shock. Hermia's hatred of Demetrius parallels his loathing of Helena, again adding continuity to the text. Notice how carefully Shakespeare has structured his play; by repeating key images, such as the moon or the serpent or Cupid's arrow, and key relationships and feelings, he has created a fluid, continuous text.

Theme

The relationship of Hermia and Helena is also parallel with that of Titania and her Indian votress. Like Titania and her friend, Helena and Hermia are as close as sisters. Together they sang with one voice, often working as if their hands and minds were united. Indeed, Helena compares them to a "double cherry" that seems to be parted, yet is united at the stem. Close friendship is another form of love exalted in this play. Helena chides her friend for destroying this ancient bond for the sake of a man; not only is this action a treachery against Helena, but it is an injury against all women. Of course, Helena here forgets that she has also done Hermia wrong; she told Demetrius about her friend's plan of elopement as a ploy to win his love, despite the fact that such knowledge might not be beneficial to Hermia. The play shows the conflicts that often ensue between love and friendship. For women in particular, friendship appears to be a vital part of life. Both Titania's actions with the Indian boy and Helena's comments in this scene suggest that women need to stick together, supporting each other, rather than letting their love for a man destroy their bonds of friendship. While the tides of love are forever ebbing and flowing, the waves of true friendship are calm and constant.

Such a friendship does not exist between Lysander and Demetrius. Although the text presents enough detail about the women's appearances and personalities for the reader to differentiate them, the two male lovers are basically indistinguishable. Both Lysander and Demetrius are critiqued for their fickle, faithless ways, and Helena criticizes them further for their unmanly behavior toward her. Suggesting that they are men only "in show," Helena argues that real men would not mock a lady, would not pretend to love her when they actually hate her. Making a woman cry does not qualify as "a manly enterprise" in Helena's opinion. What are the attributes of a gentleman? For Helena, honesty and faithfulness seem to be the two primary requirements. Neither she nor Hermia provides any explanation for their love of Demetrius and Lysander, respectively. No mention is made of either man's appearance or of any special aspects of his personality, so there seems to be no reason for either woman's love. Indeed, the similarities in Demetrius' and Lysander's personalities become pronounced as they run through the fog Puck creates to keep them from fighting. Puck speaks with both their voices, so together the three generate a melange of voices in which individual identities are completely lost.

Do we see changes in the personalities of Puck or Oberon in this scene? From the beginning of the play, Puck has been presented as a mischievous elf, toying with the people in the surrounding villages to create entertainment for Oberon. His playful side is also emphasized here. As the scene opens, he revels in relating to Oberon the effects of his transformation of Bottom into an ass. Not only did Titania fall in love with the monstrous fellow, but Bottom's friends were so frightened by the change that they felt the entire woods had been transformed into something malevolent, so that even the briars and branches maliciously tore their clothing. When he realizes that he's placed the love potion into the wrong Athenian's eyes and that soon two men will be chasing after Helena, he is excited by the "sport," preferring things that happen "prepost'rously" (121). In addition, he does not accept the blame for this mistake but labels it an act of fate. Similarly, he blames Cupid, rather than himself, for making "poor females mad" (441). Mischief and chaos are Puck's domain.

Oberon, on the other hand, is a more responsible fairy. The ruler of the fairy world, Oberon is not pleased to learn that Puck has charmed the wrong Athenian. On the one hand, Oberon's behavior towards Titania is imperious and self-serving: He is delighted that she has fallen for an ass. Yet he is not interested in creating havoc solely for his own amusement, as is Puck. Instead, he would like to make false loves turn true, promoting joy and love in the world. Oberon also reveals that he is not one of the "damned spirits" who haunts the world by night. He is a different type of spirit, one that enjoys the morning, the fiery-red sun. While literature abounds with malevolent fairies who vex humanity, Oberon and his crew are benevolent creatures, promoting peace and happiness in the human realm.

Glossary

patches (9) clowns.

noll (17) head.

mimic (19) burlesque actor.

russet-pated choughs (21) reddish brown-headed crows.

Antipodes (55) the opposite side of the earth.

mispris'd (74) mistaken.

fancy-sick (96) lovesick.

Taurus (141) mountain range along the S coast of Asia Minor, Turkey.

Ethiope (257) a black person; a reference to Hermia's relatively dark hair and complexion.

cankerblossom (282) a worm that destroys the flower bud.

minimus (329) petite person.

coil (339) commotion; turmoil.

aby (335) to pay the penalty for.

welkin (356) the vault of heaven, the sky, or the upper air.

Acheron (357) a river in Hades: often identified as the river across which Charon ferries the dead.

Aurora's harbinger (380) the morning star, precursor of the dawn.

the Morning's love (389) Cephalus, a beautiful boy loved by Aurora.

recreant (409) cowardly, craven.

wot (422) to know.

Act IV, Scene 1

Summary

Bottom is enjoying his sojourn in Titania's bower: Peaseblossom amiably scratches his head, while Cobweb goes off in search of honey for him. As Bottom sleeps in Titania's arms, Oberon walks in. Feeling pity for Titania's pitiful love for this ass, Oberon squeezes an herb on her eyes to release her from the spell. Titania awakens, telling Oberon about her strange dream of being in love with an ass. Oberon has Puck remove the ass' head from Bottom. Now that Oberon has won the Indian boy from Titania, he is willing to forget their argument, and the two, reunited, dance off together so they can bless Theseus' marriage.

Theseus, Hippolyta, and Egeus are walking through the woods when Theseus suddenly spies the sleeping lovers. Egeus recognizes them but wonders how they ended up together because Demetrius and Lysander are enemies. Theseus imagines they woke early to observe the rite of May and remembers this is the day Hermia needs to make a choice about her future. When the lovers are awakened, Demetrius confesses that he now loves Helena. No one really understands what has happened. Theseus decides the lovers should be married along with him and Hippolyta.

As the lovers return to the palace, the scene shifts to Bottom. Just awakening from his dream, Bottom declares he'll have Quince write a ballad about it, called "Bottom's Dream," because it has no bottom.

Commentary

Titania and Bottom continue to be entertaining because of the discrepancy in their modes of thinking, a difference that could be ascribed not only to their species (fairy versus human), but also to their classes. When Titania offers Bottom the soothing music provided by her fairies, he prefers the more rustic entertainment of the "tongs and the bones." When she offers him whatever food he desires, he chooses the simple fare of oats and hay. When he prosaically feels an "exposition" of sleep coming on, a malapropism for "disposition," she poetically promises to "entwist" him, much as the female ivy "[e]nrings" the barky elm. While the contrast between these two lovers contributes to the comedy of the play, it also serves Shakespeare's purpose of reminding us that love is blind and possibly deaf. Just like this mismatched couple, love often pairs seemingly inappropriate people.

Character Insight

Often played by the same actor, the two rulers in the play, Oberon and Theseus, both insist on getting their way, but they also have a benevolent side. Theseus, for example, offered Hermia the opportunity of living in a nunnery if she didn't marry Demetrius, unlike her father, who offered her only death. Thus, Theseus insists she follow her father's rules yet also offers a more lenient, more appropriate punishment. Similarly, Oberon shows his compassion for humanity by helping Helena when she is tormented by Demetrius. He also has goodwill for Titania, despite their fighting. Although Oberon initially enjoyed her inappropriate love for Bottom, he soon begins to pity Titania. Although he self-servingly releases her from the love spell only after he has won the Indian boy, Oberon seems genuinely pleased when he and Titania are reunited.

Egeus, on the other hand, seems to be an unacceptable model of authority; while he earlier was willing to send his daughter to death because of her refusal to marry the man he has seemingly arbitrarily chosen for her, here he is equally anxious to condemn Lysander to death for his disobedience. For Egeus, life is a game, and he is angry primarily because the lovers have "defeated him." Hatred and winning are more important to him than love. Therefore, Theseus overrules him, demanding not death from Lysander, but marriage—Theseus, like Oberon, participates in the triumph of love within the play.

A climax has been reached in the play's action, and it now moves toward a happy ending. Like the moon, the play has come full circle, so a new round can begin. This fresh round commences with a reunion of Titania and Oberon, who will spread prosperity and faith to all of the lovers in the play. The next accord is discovered when Theseus and Hippolyta find the four lovers sleeping in the woods.

Literary Device

Before the lovers are discovered, however, the interchange between Theseus and Hippolyta uses the imagery of hunting. The musical baying of Theseus' dogs competes for dominance with the music of Titania and Oberon's fairies, creating a "musical confusion" (109). Hippolyta has also come full circle; although the other characters remember her feats as a warrior, the opening scene of the play presented her as passive, almost silent. Here she reminisces with Theseus about her feats with Hercules and Cadmus, reminding him of her past feats as a hunter. The disjunction between these stories of war and the sight of the four lovers asleep in their bower seems jarring.

Theme

Why would Shakespeare move so quickly from a discussion of a violent hunt to an image of innocent love? Remember that the surface of this seemingly romantic play has been riddled with violence, from Egeus' wish to have his daughter killed for disobedience to Demetrius' promise to rape Helena if she did not stop pursuing him. Even Helena's images of taking the masculine role of Apollo carried a trace of rape and violation, as they evoked Apollo's violent attempt on Daphne's innocence. In some sense, the play seems to suggest that love and violence are closely aligned; as a pursuit, marriage is a game of domination and control. For example, Theseus and Hippolyta's marriage is not based on an innocent game of romance; instead, she is a prisoner of war, the quarry Theseus won with his sword.

In this play, humanity's animal nature is never far from sight—Bottom is transformed into an animal, or perhaps his true self is simply allowed to shine through. Even Titania, a seemingly regal and poetic creature, has an animal side, as shown by her love affair with Bottom. In suggesting that the lovers have come to the woods to celebrate the rites of May (a ritual of sex and fertility), Theseus seems to suggest the often purifying effects of such rituals; by allowing the lovers to access their animal sides, their anger and jealousy have been cleansed, and they can now sleep harmoniously side by side.

Waking from their dream in the woods, the lovers cannot remember how they ended up together. Lysander cannot say where he is, showing the inadequacy of language to capture the magical experiences of the woods, just as Demetrius cannot understand what power melted his love for Hermia. Like love itself, the events of the previous evening occurred in a magical zone beyond the realm of human speech or of human understanding. Although Oberon told Puck to erase all their memories of the previous evening, the lovers retain some recollection of their night in the forest. And the love spell is never removed from Demetrius' eyes, emphasizing that the walls separating reality and imagination, sleep and waking mesh to create a new version of reality. Demetrius is the sole character in the play who is punished, so it seems that hard-heartedness is the only unacceptable fault. The true lovers are rewarded, including Helena, who gets her man.

**Style &
Language**

In describing his newly rekindled love for Helena, Demetrius uses much the same language Lysander used in Act III, Scene 1, again emphasizing the similarities between the two lovers. Like Lysander, Demetrius sees his love for Hermia as a remnant of childhood, an "idle gaud" he must discard as he enters adulthood. Similarly, his love for Helena resides primarily in his eyes, of which she is the "object and pleasure" (169). He adds the imagery of disease to Lysander's formula: His love of Hermia was a sickness that caused him to lose his appetite for his natural food. Now his true appetite, Helena, has been regained. His language shows the hunger, the lust, that underlies and accompanies romantic relationships. Yet Helena is aware of the discrepancy in Demetrius' character, claiming he is her own, but not her own. Love is so much like a dream that she cannot believe in its reality, nor can any of the other lovers.

Waking from his adventures in the fairy realm, Bottom also has trouble differentiating reality and illusion. In a moment of wisdom, Bottom realizes that his dream is past the "wit of man to say what dream it was" (204); as the lovers discovered earlier in this scene, dreams and visions are often untellable. Indeed, Bottom believes men are asses if they try to explain this dream—not every event of life is amenable to rational explanation, and some things exist most fully in the realm of the imagination. According to Bottom, such visionary experiences cannot be comprehended by any of the human senses: not eyes, not ears, not hands, not tongues, not hearts. Only art, literature, can capture these magical, visionary experiences, so Bottom will have Peter Quince write a ballad about his night with the fairies.

Bottom decides to title this piece "Bottom's Dream" because it has no bottom—all literature and art are bottomless, in that their meaning cannot be quantified, cannot be understood solely through the mechanisms of reason or logic. Instead, they must be experienced, must be felt, an interchange that happens between a reader and a text. Although literary critics or other writers may try to guide a reader's responses to a text, each reader must create his or her own vision, limited only by imagination. And an individual's reading of a text will change with the reader's experience. Your first reading of *A Midsummer Night's Dream* will not be the same as your twentieth, because your life and circumstances will influence what you notice and how you interpret the play. Thus, the possible interpretations of any piece of literature are infinite and, therefore, bottomless.

The scene ends not only with this vision of infinity, but also with a mystery. In his final line, Bottom exclaims that he will sing his ballad "at her death," but who is this "her"? Is Bottom referring to Titania? To Elizabeth? We don't know. Again, a gap exists in the text in which the reader must position him- or herself to create a unique reading of the play.

Glossary

coy (2) caress.

neaf (16) fist.

tong & bones (25) instruments for rustic music.

peck of provender (27) one-quarter bushel of grain.

bottle of hay (28) bundle of hay.

exposition of (33) Bottom's malapropism for "disposition to."

vaward (100) vanguard.

Cadmus (107) a Phoenician prince and founder of Thebes: he killed a dragon and sowed its teeth, from which many armed men rose, fighting each other, until only five were left to help him build the city.

hounds of Sparta (109) dogs famous for their hunting skill.

Thessalian (117) inhabitant of Thessaly, a region of E Greece, between the Pindus Mountains and the Aegean Sea.

St. Valentine (134) birds were supposed to choose mates on St. Valentine's Day.

idle gaud (162) useless trinket.

patched (202) wearing motley (many-colored garments).

Act IV, Scene 2

Summary

In this short scene, Quince and Flute are searching for their missing friend, Bottom. They worry that "Pyramus and Thisbe" won't be performed without him. Theseus is known for his generosity, and the actors believe they will potentially be rewarded with a lifelong pension for their stellar performance of this play. As they lament this lost opportunity, Bottom suddenly returns. His friends want to hear his story, but Bottom tells them there isn't time for that now: They must prepare for the play. He warns them to avoid onions and garlic so their breath will be sweet for the "sweet comedy" they will perform.

Commentary

Bottom's friends believe he has been, according to Starveling, "transported." His word choice conflates two meanings: metamorphosed and carried away. As the audience knows, Bottom was indeed carried away by Titania and is the only mortal other than the Indian boy who has successfully penetrated the fairies' bower. Transported is also a word associated with drama, describing the elation and otherworldliness an audience feels when viewing a particularly moving dramatic performance. Like Bottom, the audience of this *Dream* should be transported into a dream world, transformed by the magical performance unfolding in the theater. The actors feel that only Bottom has the correct attributes to have this type of impact on the audience. Only he can correctly personify Pyramus because of his wit, his good looks, and his sweet voice.

Style & Language

Once again, the actors' incorrect use of language adds a comic element to the play. Quince claims Bottom is a "very paramour for a sweet voice," but Flute recognizes the error in his statement. He corrects Quince, explaining that "paragon" is the word he should have used, and that a paramour is something shameful. Flute is correct, but in some sense so is Quince. Bottom was involved in an illicit relationship with Titania, so he warrants the title of paramour, and his "sweet voice," his singing, is what first attracted her to him. Much of the humor in this exchange hinges on the layers of meaning hidden in each incorrect word used; in fact, the improper words contain more meaning than the correct ones because they expand the audience's sense of the truth. Unlike Quince and Flute, for example, we know that Bottom has been a paramour, so this word actually accounts for more of our experience of the play than Flute's more technically correct "paragon." In fact, Bottom seems to be a paragon, or shining example, only of an ass.

Like Bottom, the captive audience may be left tongue-tied, without the words to describe their experience. Bottom recognizes that he has been part of a wondrous event, yet he cannot explain what it was. Like a dream, his memories of his time in Titania's bower fade as soon as he returns to his everyday world. When Quince asks for the tale, Bottom cannot utter a word. Instead, he discourses about the upcoming performance of "Pyramus and Thisbe," reminding the actors of the mundane activities they must accomplish to make their efforts a success: Thisbe must have clean clothes, the lion should not cut his fingernails because they need to resemble claws, and so on. Once again, Bottom sticks with the bottom-line, with the real, mundane tasks. Discoursing about dreams, speaking in Titania's poetical language, are not Bottom's strengths; instead, he's a key voice of commonsense.

Glossary

transported (2) carried off by the fairies, or transformed.

strings to your beards (26) the actors used strings to tie their false beards on.

preferred (28) presented for acceptance.

Act V, Scene 1

Summary

The play has come full circle, and the cast has now returned to the palace where Theseus and Hippolyta discuss the strange tale the lovers have told them about the events of the previous evening. The joyous lovers enter, and Theseus decides it is time to plan the festivities for the evening. Of all the possible performances, the play "Pyramus and Thisbe" turns out to be the most promising. Theseus is intrigued by the paradoxical summary of the play, which suggests it is both merry and tragical, tedious and brief. Philostrate tries to dissuade Theseus from choosing this play, but Theseus thinks its simplicity will be refreshing.

In the remainder of the scene, the players present "Pyramus and Thisbe," accompanied by the lovers' critical commentary. Hippolyta is disgusted by this pathetic acting, but Theseus argues that even the best actors create only a brief illusion; the worst must be assisted by an imaginative audience. Following the performance, Bottom arises from the dead, asking Theseus if he'd like to hear an epilogue or watch a rustic dance. Theseus opts for the dance, having lost patience with the players' acting.

The play concludes with three epilogues. The first is Puck's poetic monologue, delivered while he sweeps up the stage. Oberon and Titania offer their blessing on the house and on the lovers' future children. The play ends with Puck's final speech, in which he apologizes for the weakness of the performance and promises that the next production will be better.

Commentary

After hearing the report of the lovers about their night in the woods, Hippolyta believes that something truly "strange" has occurred. Theseus accepts that the stories are strange but doesn't think they are true. He famously creates a connection between the imaginations of lovers, lunatics, and poets: All three see beyond the limitation of "cool reason"; all are beset by fantasies. While the lunatic's imagination makes heaven into a hell, the lover's shapes beauty in the ugliest face. The poet, meanwhile, creates entire worlds from the "airy nothing" of imagintion. In Theseus' opinion, all of the fantasies lack the stamp of truth, but Hippolyta is not convinced. Because all of the lovers tell the same story, she believes their tale, despite its seemingly fantastical attributes. Thseus is primarily the voice of reason, logic, law in the text, while Hippolyta valorizes the fantastic and imaginary as equally valid versions of the truth.

Yet Theseus also has a penchant for the absurd. He chooses the play of "Pyramus and Thisbe" as the entertainment for the post-wedding festivities because of its paradoxical nature. As discussed earlier, the play is billed as "tedious brief" and also "tragical mirth." Theseus wonders about this discordant assortment of adjectives, calling the play "hot ice" and "wondrous strange snow." Philostrate, the Master of Revels, warns Theseus that the play is "nothing," but even such bottomless entertainments, as "Bottom's Dream" showed, are something. Theseus is particularly impressed that the play will be performed by working-class actors. For him, the simpleness and sincerity of their efforts make nothing into something; the content is less important than the intentions of the actors.

Another rift exists here between Theseus and Hippolyta. While he feels that the actors' intentions are key, she does not think sincerity can make up for these amateur actors' lack of talent. Theseus disagrees, arguing that it is the audience's duty to recognize the actors' intentions. Is Theseus being kindhearted and egalitarian here or is he patronizing these lower-class actors? This is a question for the reader to answer, based on the details presented in the play, together with his or her experience of the world. Some readers might believe he is patronizing both the amateur actors and his new bride.

The Prologue of the play-within-the-play justifies Philostrate's lukewarm recommendation. Throughout this drama, Shakespeare has panned the acting crew's misuse of the English language, and here Quince's incorrect punctuation adds humor. For example, his opening line, "If we offend, it is with our good will," suggests the actors are intentionally offending their audience. Although he would like to tell the audience that he and the other actors plan to please the court, his Prologue suggests just the opposite meaning. Quince's errors should remind all writers of the importance of good grammar and punctuation; without them, meaning becomes twisted, even, as in this case, comically reversed. Here is a correctly punctuated version of the speech that more accurately captures Quince's intentions:

If we offend, it is with our good will
That you should think we come, not to offend,
But with good will to show our simple skill—
That is the true beginning of our end.
Consider then we come—but in despite
We do not come—as minding to content you.
Our true intent is all for your delight:
We are not here that you should here repent you
The actors are at hand and, by their show,
You shall know all that you are like to know.

As Lysander says, it isn't enough to speak; one must also speak correctly, a good lesson for all readers of this drama. For Hippolyta, Quince sounds like a child trying to play a recorder, and even Theseus recognizes the disorder in Quince's language.

The play provides numerous lessons for writers. For example, the comedy of Pyramus' opening speech lies in the overabundance of "O"s and "alack"s that Bottom adds to the text. While Bottom hopes this poetical language will intensify the seriousness of his speech, its excess adds comedy rather than tragedy. Rather than adding meaning, such shallow poetical devices detract from the play by drawing attention to themselves rather than highlighting the tragedy of Pyramus' plight. Bottom's improvisation also shows would-be screenwriters that piles of adjectives detract from meaning; for example, Bottom's, "O wall, O sweet and lovely wall," seems merely ridiculous. Simple, unadorned language would have more impact.

As expected, the play is absurdly comical, and the humor is intensified by the audience's interactions with the cast. After Snout explains his role as a wall, Theseus sincerely wonders if "lime and hair," the ingredients that make a wall, could ever speak better, and Demetrius claims Snout to be the wittiest wall he has ever heard. Bottom's matter-of-fact approach to life is apparent once again as he converses with Theseus during the play. When Theseus suggests that the wall should curse, Bottom replies that it shouldn't. Bottom is unable to recognize the joke in Theseus' statement because he believes the audience is completely transported by the play. Despite his criticism of the play, Theseus argues that the best actors are mere shadows, as are the worst, if the audience's imagination guides them. Again, he feels the audience should recognize the actors' intentions, rather than focus entirely on their production. In a final crack at the play, Theseus believes the ending would have been improved if Pyramus had hanged himself with Thisbe's garter, but, overall, the play was entertaining—even though the drama was obviously uncouth, it still "beguil'd / The heavy gait of night."

The play ends by juxtaposing three epilogues with very different moods. From the comedy of Pyramus and Thisbe, the scene shifts to Puck's first, fairly ominous epilogue. As he sweeps away the stage, Puck invokes the dangerous creatures of the night: roaring lions, howling wolves, and graveyard spirits. Day is juxtaposed with night, marriage with death. But the play doesn't end here. Oberon reinvokes the light, asking the "drowsy fire" to glimmer throughout the house. While Puck's fairies were night creatures, "[f]ollowing darkness like a dream," Oberon's are light as birds, dancing and singing as they "tripplingly" follow him. Like the ever-changing moon, the play's moods and emotions keep shifting, emphasizing life's multidimensionality. Puck and Oberon invoke different versions of the nighttime world, and both exist, both are relevant. While Puck provides a *memento mori,* reminding the audience that death is howling just around the corner, Oberon brings joy and blessing into our lives for as long as they last. In his blessing for the newlyweds, Oberon offers them long-lasting love and exorcises any blots of nature that could desecrate their children. With peace and safety, he consecrates the palace itself.

Oberon's final speech seems an apt place to end the play, especially if it was, indeed, performed for a wedding celebration, but Shakespeare does not stop here. Significantly the final words of the play do not belong to the ruler of the fairy realm, but to the master of misrule, the consummate actor and comedian, Puck. In some sense, Puck, with his ability to translate himself into any character, with his skill in creating performances that seem all too real to their human audiences, could be seen as a mascot of the theater. Therefore, his final words are an apology for the play itself. Like the lovers in the play, the audience of the *Dream* has also been treated to a vision. If this performance has not met the audience's expectations, the actors will practice more and improve their work.

Glossary

brow of Egypt (11) face of a gypsy.

abridgement (39) pastime.

Bacchanals (48) worshippers of Bacchus, the god of wine and revelry.

Thracian (49) belonging to an ancient region in the E Balkan Peninsula.

conn'd (80) to peruse carefully; to study; fix in the memory.

stand upon points (118) pay attention to details.

hight (138) named; called.

Limander, Helen (190, 191) blunders for the lovers Hero and Leander; Leander swims the Hellespont from Abydos every night to be with her; when he drowns in a storm, Hero throws herself into the sea.

Shafalus and Procrus (192) blunders for "Cephalus" and "Procris," famous lovers.

'tide (197) betide; happen.

Furies (266) the three terrible female spirits with snaky hair (Alecto, Tisiphone, and Megaera) who punish the doers of unavenged crimes.

thread and thrum (268) everything, both good and bad.

mote (299) a speck of dust or other tiny particle.

videlicet (303) that is, namely.

Sisters Three (316) the Fates, the three goddesses who control human destiny and life.

imbrue (324) stain.

Bergomask dance (332) a rustic dance, named for Bergamo (a province ridiculed for its rusticity).

wasted brands (351) burned-out logs.

triple Hecate's team (360) Hecate, a goddess of the moon (Luna), earth (Diana), and underground realm of the dead (Hecate), later regarded as the goddess of sorcery and witchcraft.

CHARACTER ANALYSES

Hermia

Critics often recognize the similarity between Hermia and Helena because both represent the difficulties of adolescent love. But these two young women are more different than their male counterparts, Lysander and Demetrius, who are, indeed, indistinguishable. Not only do these two young women show the trials and tribulations of young love, but their interactions emphasize the importance of female friendship and the gender expectations that often make women's lives difficult. As the play opens, Hermia is under trial. Her father insists she marry Demetrius, the man he prefers, rather than Lysander, the man she loves. Her father reminds the audience that Hermia has no choice in this matter: Hermia is his property, and the laws declare he can dispose of her as he wishes, even if this means sending her to her death. Theseus agrees: According to him, Hermia's father should be a god to her. She is merely a form in wax that has been imprinted with her father's power. Even though Theseus offers her the choice of living in a nunnery rather than dying, he won't allow her to make her own decision about a husband. Her "fancy" conflicts with her father's "will," emphasizing that an adolescent girl has no power against the will of law.

Later in the play, Hermia is criticized for her being "dark," an Ethiope, in contrast with "light" Helena's blondeness. Hermia's "darkness" is significant, reminding us of the racial slurs that continue to plague our culture. Similarly, her fears that Lysander has abandoned her because she's shorter than Helena show that body image issues aren't a recent problem for women: Even in the sixteenth century, women equated build with desirability, often discovering themselves on the short end of this stick. Hermia's belief that Lysander has deserted her because of her body type also emphasizes the fickleness of love, which is often based not on deep features of character, but on trivial aspects of appearance.

Helena

Obsessed over Demetrius, Helena's character emphasizes the capriciousness of love and its excesses. Even though she knows she is making a fool of herself by pursuing Demetrius, Helena cannot stop the chase. She reminds us that love is blind, declaring that she is as beautiful as Hermia, so there is no logical explanation for Demetrius' sudden shift in affection. This point is further emphasized by the two men's love potion-induced attraction for her. Through these interactions, we learn that love is blind, illogical, seemingly produced by magic's sleight-of-hand, rather than reason's honesty. Like a child, lovers are often beguiled by trivial trinkets rather than deep character traits. This message is further heightened by the blandness of Lysander and Demetrius. As Lysander makes clear in his conversation with Egeus in Act I, no noticeable differences exist between the two men, so Helena could just as easily love one as the other.

Besides emphasizing love's arbitrary nature, Helena also highlights the gender differences that vex women. Unlike men who can woo whomever they please, women are not allowed to fight for love; instead, they must passively wait for the man of their dreams to notice them. In chasing Demetrius through the woods, Helena is breaking the rules of her sex, becoming the pursuer rather than the pursued. She likens herself to Apollo who chased the unwilling huntress Daphne through the woods. Helena's choice of examples is significant because it emphasizes the violence men (or gods in this case) have often perpetrated against women: Apollo wanted not only to capture Daphne, but to rape her. In chasing Demetrius, Helena claims to have appropriated Apollo's role, yet Demetrius is still the one who threatens violence when he vows to "do [her] mischief in the wood" if she doesn't stop following him. Not only must woman patiently wait for her chosen lover to call, but she is also constantly threatened by male sexual violence if she resists unwanted male attentions.

What recourse do women have? Banding together. Thus, Helena is upset when she believes Hermia has betrayed her by joining Demetrius and Lysander. Childhood friendships between women should be stronger than the fickle love of men. Her comments make us question the position of all women in the play. For example, what is the source of Hippolyta's passivity in the play? Like Daphne, she has been captured and ravished by a male warrior. Did she lose her power when she lost the society of other women? And what about Titania? Why isn't she angry upon discovering that Oberon has charmed her and stolen her precious Indian boy? By focusing on these instances of male violence, the play implicitly suggests that women should become more active. Notice that Helena, who has actively pursued Demetrius, is rewarded for her proactive pursuit.

Bottom

Probably created as a showcase for one of Shakespeare's favorite actors, Bottom's role involves dancing, singing, and laughter. From his first introduction, Bottom is presented as courageous and outgoing. He is confident in his ability to play any, even all, roles in "Pyramus and Thisbe." For example, he says his performance of Pyramus will cause the audience to cry a stormload of tears. As the audience realizes, this confidence is misplaced, and Bottom is little more than a swaggering fool—indeed, an ass, as Puck's prank makes apparent.

Bottom's language adds to his comic appeal. For example, he claims that if he performed the role of Thisbe, he would speak her lines in a "monstrous little voice," an obviously contradictory statement. Then he would "aggravate" his voice if he played the lion's role so that the ladies in the audience would not be frightened; once again, Bottom's word choices show his silliness, while adding a comic element to the play. Similarly, rather than worry about his acting performance, Bottom wonders which beard would be most effective for the role of Pyramus.

Although Bottom is the locus of comedy in the play—he's a traditional Shakespearean clown—he also draws the audience's attention to serious themes, such as the relationship between reality and imagination. In preparing for the performance of "Pyramus and Thisbe," Bottom continually draws his fellow players' attention back to the question of the audience's gullibility: Will the ladies be upset when Pyrmus kills himself; will they realize that the lion is not a lion but an actor? To remedy the first problem, Bottom asks Quince to write a prologue, explaining Pyramus is not really dead, and that Pyramus is not, in fact, Pyramus, but Bottom the weaver. In this instance, Bottom focuses the audience's attention on the difficulty of differentiating reality and perception; his solution suggests his belief that the players' acting will be too convincing, that they will fully realize the goal of theater. Similarly, to keep the ladies from being afraid of the lion, he suggests the actor playing the lion show half of his face and explain that he's really a man, not an animal. This belief in the power of theater extends to his solutions for bringing moonshine and a wall into the play. In creating a wall for the set, he believes covering a man with plaster and some loam will sufficiently convince an audience. Always ready to be surprised, to accept the world's wonder, Bottom believes his audience will be equally susceptible to the powers of art.

Bottom's openness to the world's oddities extends to his visit to the fairy realm, which could be viewed as simply another fantasy, much like the theater. It is ironic that Bottom, the most down-to-earth character in the play, is the only mortal who meets any of the fairies. When Titania falls in love with him, Bottom isn't surprised. But he does recognize that Titania's statements about him aren't true, for example that he is an angel or that his looks inspire confidence. At bottom, he knows love and reason don't often work at the same level. Once again, his comments focus on a key, recurring theme of the play: How do love and reason relate? Should love be based on reason or on fantasy? In addition, Bottom's interactions with Titania emphasize the class differences between the characters in the play; as a member of the artisan class, Bottom was literally in a different realm from the regal Queen of the Fairies.

When he returns to the real world, following his stay in the fairy world, Bottom would like to discuss his experiences. He can't. Although he usually is full of language, he is unable to speak about his fairy-inspired visions. Instead, he wants Peter Quince to write a ballad about these experiences; what ordinary language cannot accommodate, poetic language can. Unlike Theseus, Bottom has complete faith in the power of art to capture visionary experiences. Through him, Shakespeare implicitly validates the vision of the artist.

Puck

Oberon's jester and lieutenant, Puck is a powerful supernatural creature, capable of circling the globe in 40 minutes or of enshrouding unsuspecting mortals in a deep fog. Also known as Robin Goodfellow, Puck would have been familiar to a sixteenth-century English audience, who would have recognized him as a common household spirit also often associated with travelers. But he's also a "puck," an elf or goblin that enjoys playing practical jokes on mortals. Although he is more mischievous than malevolent, Puck reminds us that the fairy world is not all goodness and generosity.

Another definition of his name aligns him with a Norse demon, sometimes associated with the devil. Perhaps it isn't surprising that he brings a somewhat more dangerous element to Titania and Oberon's seemingly benevolent fairy realm. He invokes the "damned spirits" that wander home to graveyards after a night of evil doing, while Oberon reminds him that his band of fairies are aligned with the morning dew, with sunlight and joy. Unlike Oberon who genuinely tries to create human happiness, Puck seems indifferent to human suffering. When he has accidentally caused both Lysander and Demetrius to fall in love with Helena, Puck enjoys the pleasure their folly brings him. Although he restores the proper lovers to each other, he does so only at Oberon's request, not out of any feelings of remorse. Similarly, Oberon feels repentance for Titania's idiotic love for Bottom, but Puck doesn't. While Oberon and Titania bless the newlyweds in Act V, Puck reminds the audience of the dangers of the night, graves gaping open and wolves howling at the moon. As a traditional Shakespearean fool, Puck makes us aware of the darker side of life, the underworld realm of shadows and magic and, ultimately, death.

Oberon

The King of the Fairies, Oberon's personality has two sides. On the one hand, he ensures that the proper lovers end up together by the end of the play. He sympathizes with the sorely abused Helena and causes Demetrius to fall madly in love with her. As a benevolent ruler of the spirit world, he also brings blessing of peace and health to the future families of the newlyweds. But his personality is not all kindness; Oberon shows a more malicious side in his dealings with Titania.

Their initial interaction in the play begins with a fight. The dual has been brought about by Titania's possession of an Indian boy. While Titania appears to be legitimately raising this child, the only son of one of her votresses who died in childbirth, Oberon has decided he wants the boy as a servant. Why? Shakespeare never tells us. Perhaps Oberon wants to prove his male authority over Titania; perhaps he feels Titania is overindulging the boy and would like to bring discipline into his life. Any explanation the audience comes up with must be based in conjecture, because Shakespeare does not explain Oberon's motivation. No explanation, though, would seem to justify the cruelty Oberon uses in winning the boy away from Titania. Oberon casts a spell upon her, a trick that leaves her in love with Bottom, the ass. Many critics recognize Oberon's kindness in releasing her from this spell as soon as he has gotten what he wanted from her—the boy—but his treachery must still be acknowledged.

Theseus

Like Oberon, Theseus is a contradictory character. On the one hand, he is the ruler of Athens and represents the voice of law and authority in the mortal realm, paralleling Oberon's similar position in the fairy world. His duty as dispenser of justice is seen early in the play through his interaction with Hermia and Egeus. Although Theseus is more understanding of Hermia's situation than her father, he still vows to sentence her to death if she won't accept one of his two alternatives: marrying Demetrius or entering a convent. Even when Hippolyta is noticeably upset with his verdict, Theseus insists that a daughter's first goal must be to obey her father. As upholder of authority in Athens, Theseus' first duty is to support the city's laws, even when they appear unfair.

Based on this example, Theseus' view of love would seem to fit within the boundaries of law and reason. This notion is supported by his speech at the beginning of Act V, in which he famously announces that the imaginations of poets, madmen, and lovers are all the same: All are prone to excesses beyond the realm of reason. But isn't Theseus also a lover? His statement seems to discount his own position as lover of Hippolyta; as a reasonable man, does he qualify as a lover? Yet even the rational Theseus claims time moves too slowly as he anticipates his wedding day, showing his unreasonable longing. But his love for Hippolyta is not the pure, fresh, freely chosen affection of Hermia and Lysander. As Theseus reminds his bride, he won her by doing her harm: She was part of the spoils of war. In their quarrel, Oberon and Titania tell us this is not the first relationship for either Hippolyta or Theseus. Not only has Theseus' name been linked with Titania's, but he has supposedly ravished and deserted Perigouna, Ariadne, and Antiope, among others. Similarly, Hippolyta has been the "buskin'd mistress" of Oberon and has spent time with Hercules and Cadmus. Not lovers in their first bloom, Theseus and Hippolyta offer a picture of more mature love.

Theseus' famous speech from Act V also appears to denigrate the poet's imaginative faculty by aligning him with lovers and madmen. He argues that the poet "gives to airy nothing / A local habitation and a name," a trick performed by strong imaginations. His theory denies the importance of craft and discipline in the creation of art, casting artistic talent as little more than airy fantasy. In choosing a play for the wedding festivities, he does not select the most skillful performers, but those who present their art with simplicity, duty, and modesty. While Hippolyta dislikes the silly performance of the players, Theseus argues that both good and bad actors create but "shadows," and the audience must flesh out the performances through their own imaginations. Overall, Theseus' view of imagination minimizes the work of the artist, placing more responsibility on the audience.

CRITICAL ESSAYS

"A Silver Bow, New Bent in Heaven": Moon Imagery in *A Midsummer Night's Dream*

With four separate plots and four sets of characters, *A Midsummer Night's Dream* risks fragmentation. Yet Shakespeare has managed to create a unified play through repetition of common themes—such as love—and through cohesive use of imagery. Shining throughout the play, the moon is one of the primary vehicles of unity. In her inconstancy, the moon is an apt figure of the ever-changing, varied modes of love represented in the drama. As an image, the moon lights the way for all four groups of characters.

The play opens with Theseus and Hippolyta planning their wedding festivities under a moon slowly changing into her new phase—too slowly for Theseus. Like a dowager preventing him from gaining his fortune, the old moon is a crone who keeps Theseus from the bounty of his wedding day. Theseus implicitly invokes Hecate, the moon in her dark phase, the ruler of the Underworld associated with magic, mysticism, even death. This dark aspect of the moon will guide the lovers as they venture outside of the safe boundaries of Athens and into the dangerous, unpredictable world of the forest.

In this same scene, Hippolyta invokes a very different phase of the moon. Rather than the dark moon mourned by Theseus, Hippolyta imagines the moon moving quickly into her new phase, like a silver bow, bent in heaven. From stepmother, the moon is transformed in the course of a few lines into the image of fruitful union contained in the "silver bow," an implicit reference also to Cupid's arrow, which draws lovers together. Utilizing the imagery of the silver bow, Hippolyta invokes Diana, the virgin huntress who is the guardian spirit of the adolescent moon. In this guise, the moon is the patroness of all young lovers, fresh and innocent, just beginning their journey through life. This new, slender moon, though, won't last; instead, like life itself, she will move into her full maturity, into a ripe, fertile state, just as the marriages of the young lovers will grow, eventually resulting in children.

Later in the same act, the moon alters once again, returning to her role as Diana, the chaste goddess of the hunt. Theseus declares that if Hermia does not marry Demetrius as her father wishes, she will live a barren life, "[c]hanting faint hymns to the cold fruitless moon" (73). Hermia has until the next new moon to make her decision, so the new moon becomes both a symbol of Theseus and Hippolyta's happy union and of Hermia's potential withered life as a nun (or even a corpse), if she does not comply with her father's whim. In a play that celebrates love, marriage, and fertility, the chaste moon is not a welcome image. Therefore, Theseus urges Hermia to marry Demetrius, her father's choice of a husband, rather than spending a barren life in a convent. By the end of the scene, the moon presents herself in another guise: as Phoebe, the queen of moonlit forests. In this role, her "silver visage" will both light and conceal the flight of Lysander and Hermia, as they seek a happy and productive life away from the severe authority of Athens. As the play progresses, the moon will continue her transformations, accompanying all of the characters through their magical sojourns.

Guiding Theseus and Hippolyta as they prepare for their wedding, the moon also shines over the quarreling Oberon and Titania, who seek a way to patch up their failing marriage. As Oberon says when he first sees Titania, they are "ill met by moonlight." Notice how the fairy world is directly connected with the cycles of the moon: As "governess of the floods" (103), the moon, which is pale in anger because of Titania and Oberon's argument, has indirectly caused numerous human illnesses. And Titania invokes a weaker, more passive and "watery" moon that weeps along with the flowers at any violated chastity.

On a more comical level, moonshine is also relevant to the players. As they prepare their performance of "Pyramus and Thisbe," which is also drenched in moonlight, they wonder how they will manage to represent the moon. Bottom has the brilliant idea of leaving a window open during the performance so that the moon can shine in. Quince doesn't like the potential dangers of this natural solution—what if it's an overcast night—and suggests, instead, that one of the actors personify Moonshine by wearing a bush of thorns and carrying a lantern. Thus, Robin Starveling appears in the final act of the play as the Man-in-the-Moon, showing Shakespeare's dexterity in playing with all of the cultural representations that coalesce around a single image: From slender, virgin huntress to full, ripe mother to dark, mysterious crone to comical man-in-the moon, Shakespeare represents the moon in its full complexity.

Most of Shakespeare's images have similarly multiple layers of significance: Their relevance changes with their context, so no image maps simplistically onto a single meaning. Despite the multivalent meanings of the moon in this play, it is still a vehicle for unity, shining on all four groups of characters as they transform themselves in the course of the drama. Drenched in moonlight, this drama is aligned with Hecate's mystical, underworld visions; with the chaste, huntress Diana; and with Phoebe's rich fertility. But it is also aligned with the more comical, folk-loric image of the man-in-the-moon, who, in the guise of Robin Starveling the tailor, lights the action of "Pyramus and Thisbe." Part of Shakespeare's skill as a playwright was in skillfully representing all aspects of a potent cultural icon, without destroying the unity of his carefully wrought artistic creation.

Imagining Love

Exciting and new, or even tedious and worn-out, love in all its variations is presented in *A Midsummer Night's Dream*. But what is love? What causes us to fall in love? How does love relate to the world of law and reason? These questions are broached in all their complexity in Shakespeare's midsummer dream. Love is the primary concern of the play, which begins as Theseus and Hippolyta prepare for their upcoming wedding, but the picture painted of love is not necessarily romantic. Instead, the play shows the arbitrariness of desire, along with its depth, the sighs and tears that often make lovers miserable.

As Lysander tells Hermia, the course of true love never did run smooth. Often swift, short, and brief, love is besieged by class differences, by age differences, by war, by death, and by sickness. Helena's love is plagued by a different demon: indifference. The more ardently she loves Demetrius, the more thoroughly he hates her. And there seems to be no reason for his disdain: She is as beautiful as Hermia, as wealthy, as similar to Hermia as "double cherries" on a single stem. Helena's meditations present love in its guise as the childish, blindfolded Cupid, a constantly repeated image in this dream, who playfully transforms the vile into something pure and dignified. The image of blind Cupid is repeated when Titania falls in love with Bottom, the ass. Oberon's love-potion works much as Cupid's arrows are reputed to do: by impairing vision. The juice charms Titania's sight, so she is unable to see her lover for what he really is.

Love's arbitrary, irrational nature is the subject of one of Theseus' speeches. In Act V, he famously creates a connection between the imaginations of lovers, lunatics, and poets: All three see beyond the limitation of "cool reason," and all are beset by fantasies. While the lunatic's imagination makes heaven into a hell, the lover shapes beauty in the ugliest face. The poet, meanwhile, creates entire worlds from the "airy nothing" of imagination. In Theseus' opinion, all of these fantasies lack the stamp of truth; does this mean Theseus' love for Hippolyta is equally specious? The Duke would probably say no—without reasons or evidence to back up his claim—but his comments lead us deeper into the question of what constitutes love. If his love for Hippolyta is based on seemingly clear vision, what has caused him to fall in love with her rather than with someone else? A deep understanding of her personality? A reverence for her compassion or her kindness? The play doesn't tell us, but its overall logic suggests a loud "no" to both questions. In this drama, love is based entirely upon looks, upon attractiveness, or upon the love-potion that charms the eyes. Thus, for example, Hermia accounts for Lysander's surprising loss of affection by assessing her height; she is shorter and, therefore, less appealing than Helena. Like too many teenage girls in contemporary society, Hermia is plagued by doubts about her desirability. It's not surprising that body image is such a vexing issue in Western society when love is so often based on appearance, rather than essence.

Even when love is mutual and seemingly based in clear vision, it is often hampered by family disapproval. For Lysander and Hermia, love is marred by her father's desire for her to marry Demetrius. The law is on Egeus' side. All of the relationships in the play, but this one in particular, emphasize the conflict of love and law. The "ancient privilege of Athens" allows Egeus to "dispose" of his daughter as he wishes; she is his property, so he can "estate" her to anyone. His words show the violence that often supports law and points out a discord within the seeming concord of love (to paraphrase a saying of Theseus' in Act V). According to Theseus' edict, Hermia needs to fit her "fancies" to her father's "will" (I.1, 118), suggesting that Hermia's love needs to be combated by her father's authority; otherwise, the law of Athens will sacrifice her on the pyre of reason.

Yet, as noted earlier, her father's choice of Demetrius seems as fanciful and arbitrary as Hermia's choice of Lysander. Although Theseus is less willing than Theseus is to condemn Hermia to death or to celibacy, Theseus is guilty of linking violence and love: He wooed Hippolyta with a sword and won her love by "doing her injuries." Although Hippolyta seems subdued, even passive, in the play, the violence that led to their love is a constant presence. This play's representation of love is not the saccharine view presented in many modern love ballads; instead, Shakespeare returns us to our animal natures, displaying the primitive, bestial, and often violent side of human desire.

As Bottom astutely notes, reason and love keep little company with one another. The characters in this drama attempt to find a way to understand the workings of love in a rational way, yet their failures emphasize the difficulty of this endeavor. Shakespeare seems to suggest that a love potion, even though seemingly crazy, is a better way to explain the mysterious workings of sexual attraction than is common sense: Love and reason will never be friends. Nor will love ever be a controllable addiction. What fools mortals be, Puck philosophizes. And perhaps we are fools for entering into the dangerous, unpredictable world of love; yet what fun would life be without it?

A Tedious Brief Movie Review of Michael Hoffman's *A Midsummer Night's Dream*

Michael Hoffman's 1999 film version of *A Midsummer Night's Dream* transports the drama's action from ancient Athens to an imaginary Italian village named Monte Athena at the turn of the nineteenth century. In this rendition of the play, Duke Theseus isn't a conquering hero but a tired and seemingly ineffectual bureaucrat. Similarly, Hippolyta, his bride-to-be, isn't the powerful Queen of the Amazons, but a bland, yet beautiful, Victorian feminist. In transporting the play's action, Hoffman seems to have erased the drama's magic and vibrancy, leaving an insipid film, overloaded with Victorian gadgetry. As the film's opening narrative announces, bustles are out and bicycles are in; thus, the lovers chase each other madly through the woods on bicycles, their tooting horns providing a constant, jarring racket to the performance. Even the boisterous Bottom, the errant weaver, and the magical fairy kingdom have lost their charm. This film rips away the drama's magical, gossamer wings, leaving a dull, earthbound husk in their place.

Somehow this version of the play manages to disperse even Bottom's free flowing exuberance. While Shakespeare's Bottom is a bluff, self-assured, and good-hearted clown, Hoffman presents a self-conscious, easily disappointed Bottom. Kevin Kline's rendition of this working-class character seems out-of-place with his fellow working men when he arrives on the scene in a three-piece suit—gone is Bottom's sensual, down-to-earth appeal. In a scene added by Hoffman, a group of boisterous young men pour wine over Bottom as he does an impromptu performance on the street; Kline's Bottom is humiliated, rendered a laughing stock among his village folk in a self-conscious manner that doesn't fit with the play's more complex presentation of Bottom.

Another odd addition to the play is Bottom's wife. This shrewish woman judgmentally watches her husband as he performs for the crowds and disgustedly dismisses her husband following the scene in which he is drenched with wine. Once again, Hoffman creates an angst-ridden Bottom whose character does not reflect the original text.

Similarly, Hoffman's rendition of the fairy realm negates its mirth and good humor. Rather than the free-spirited lovers of life presented in the text, the fairies in the film are sniveling, petty, irritable party animals. This is especially true of Puck who has been transformed from a boyish charmer into a crass, middle-aged lounge lizard who revels in peeing in the woods after drinking too much wine. Similarly, Titania loses much of her psychological complexity in the film. The text emphasizes that the strong bonds of an ancient female friendship keep Titania from relinquishing the Indian boy—she wants to care for a dead friend's son—providing a link with the other female characters in the play, whose lives are also marked by strong friendships: Hermia and Helena are like "double cherries" on a single stem; and Hippolyta was once the leader of the Amazons, an all-female society. Hoffman eradicates this emphasis on female friendship, presenting Titania as a selfish and shrewish wife, bent on keeping the Indian boy mainly to spite Oberon.

The effect of Hoffman's changes is that the drama has lost the magic, the mystery, the mayhem of Shakespeare's original conception. Why? Movie critics agree that Hoffman missed the boat in one essential way: He didn't trust Shakespeare. Rather than allowing the language and story of the play to shine, he instead cluttered the performance with gimmicks and gadgets. Rather than letting Shakespeare's original tale tell itself, Hoffman adds scenes that add little to the play's exuberance. A key example is the mud-wrestling bout between Hermia and Helena; one trenchant critic wonders where Jerry Springer is with his whistle at this low point in the performance.

The film also fails because of its inconsistency. Many critics have noted the disparity of the acting styles within the film. A collage of American, English, and French actors, of TV stars and Shakespeareans, the variety of performance styles doesn't add up. Michelle Pfeiffer's rendition of Titania has been deemed cardboard, and many critics question her ability to deliver Shakespearean lines effectively. Even the talented Kevin Kline seems miscast as Bottom, often over performing his role, as is Rupert Everett as Oberon. The obvious clumsiness of their performances opens a critical door for the audience: Who would we cast instead in these roles? How do the director's choices match or clash with ours?

In fact these questions lead us to the film's one saving grace: It forces us to think more carefully about Shakespeare's original artistic conception. Has switching the setting from Athens to Italy enhanced our understanding of the play? Or have we lost the rich mythological resonance Shakespeare created by locating his play in Greece? Does the play's action make sense when placed in the nineteenth century; for example, does it seem plausible that Hermia would still be sentenced to death for disobedience to her father? Many of the film's choices don't seem sensible or coherent, but they make us painfully aware of the richness, the unity, the magic of Shakespeare's original text. By analyzing the details of this modern performance of the play, Shakespeare's mastery and magnetism become vividly apparent.

CliffsNotes Review

Use this CliffsNotes Review to test your understanding of the original text and reinforce what you've learned in this play. After you work through the review and essay questions, identify the quote section, and the fun and useful practice projects, you're well on your way to understanding a comprehensive and meaningful interpretation of *A Midsummer Night's Dream*.

Q&A

1. The play opens with the upcoming marriage of _____, Duke of Athens, to _____, Queen of the Amazons.

2. Two pairs of young lovers are featured in the play. The two women are Hermia, who is in love with _____, and her best friend, Helena, who is in love with _____. When the play begins, Lysander and Demetrius are both in love with _____.

3. In addition to the royals and the lovers, the play presents a group of actors who are preparing a drama called_____.

4. The craftsmen are worried that the _____ will frighten the women in the audience, and, as a result, they (the actors) might all be hanged.

5. Oberon employs a mischievous spirit as his jester and lieutenant. This spirit's name is Puck, but he is also known as _____ _____.

6. Titania and Oberon are fighting because Oberon wants custody of _____, whose mother, one of Titania's votresses, _____.

7. Stumbling upon the craftsmen rehearsing their play in the woods, Puck is amused by their poor acting skills. As a joke, he decides to turn Bottom into an _____.

8. Lysander and Demetrius both fall in love with Helena after Puck sprinkles their eyes with a love juice made from a plant called _____.

9. Helena insults Hermia by referring to her _____.

10. Puck has the final words in the play, telling the audience that if they didn't enjoy the play, they should view it as nothing but a _____.

Answers: (1) Theseus, Hippolyta. (2) Lysander, Demetrius, Hermia. (3) "The most lamentable comedy, and most cruel death of Pyramus and Thisbe." (4) lion's roar. (5) Robin Goodfellow. (6) the Indian boy, died in childbirth. (7) ass. (8) love-in-idleness. (9) diminutive stature. (10) dream.

Identify the Quote

1. Either to die the death, or to abjure
For ever the society of men.
Therefore, fair Hermia, question your desires,
Know of your youth, examine well your blood,
Whether, if you yield not to your father's choice,
You can endure the livery of a nun,
For aye to be in shady cloister mew'd,
To live a barren sister all your life,
Chanting faint hymns to the cold fruitless moon.

2. Your wrongs do set a scandal on my sex.
We cannot fight for love, as men may do;
We should be woo'd, and were not made to woo.

3. Some man or other must present Wall; and let him have some plaster, or some loam, or some rough-cast about him, to signify wall; and let him hold his fingers thus, and through that cranny shall Pyramus and Thisbe whisper.

4. These things seem small and undistinguishable,
Like far-off mountains turned into clouds.
. . . Are you sure
That we are awake? It seems to me
That yet we sleep, we dream.

5. Lovers and madmen have such seething brains,
Such shaping fantasies, that apprehend
More than cool reason ever comprehends.
The lunatic, the lover, and the poet
Are of imagination all compact.

Answers: (1) [Theseus in Act I, Scene 1, telling Hermia what her options are if she disobeys her father by refusing to marry Demetrius.] (2) [Helena in Act II, Scene 2, while following Demetrius through the woods.] (3) [Bottom in Act III, Scene 1, as the players are planning their performance of "Pyramus and Thisbe."] (4) [Demetrius, in Act IV, Scene 1, after the four lovers have awakened following their night in the woods.] (5) [Theseus in Act V, Scene 1, explaining his theory of imagination to Hipployta.]

Essay Questions

1. What is the significance of the settings of the play? What are the major characteristics of each setting (the Duke's palace, Quince's cottage, and the fairy-enchanted woods)? What significance do forests have in other literary works you're familiar with? What about urban settings? What rules and values apply in the different settings? Why is the story set in ancient Greece—would it have been as effective in contemporary England?

2. Discuss the meanings of the play's title, *A Midsummer Night's Dream*. In addition to the title, what other references do you find to dreaming in the play? What relationship is created between dreaming and theater (look, for example, at Puck's final speech)? Why is Midsummer important to the themes of the play?

3. The play presents several different couples: Theseus and Hippolyta,; Hermia and Lysander, Helena and Demetrius, Titania and Bottom, and Titania and Oberon. What aspects of love are explored in each of these relationships?

4. Gender issues are significant in this drama. What differences are there in the roles and behaviors appropriate to men and women? Do these gender differences still exist today, or are they examples of outdated stereotypes?

5. Many contemporary productions of the play cast the same actor in the role of Theseus and Oberon, and also of Hippolyta and Titania. What does this suggest about the functions of these characters in the play? How are the Hippolyta and Titania similar and/or different? Theseus and Oberon?

6. The adventures of the four young lovers—Demetrius, Lysander, Helena and Hermia—are a necessary aspect of the play, yet many critics have suggested that these four characters are "indistinguishable." Do you agree? What similarities and differences do you find among their personalities? Do you have a favorite among this group?

7. Much has been written about the darker side of this play, its savage, erotic aspects and its violence. For example, the critic Jan Kott finds the eroticism of the play "brutal." On the other hand, the critic Hartley Coleridge says this drama is "all poetry, and sweeter poetry was never written."

Which of these critics do you agree with—if either? Overall, is this a sinister, violent, erotic play or a lighthearted, romantic comedy? Support your answer with references from the text.

Practice Projects

1. This play makes many allusions to classical mythology and to Celtic fairy lore. Check out the Web site "Mythology in *A Midsummer Night's Dream*" (http://quarles.unbc.edu/midsummer/mythintro.html) to find more background on Greek and Roman mythology. How does your exploration of mythology alter your reading of the play?

2. Besides mythology, this play makes many references to nature. What plants, animals, and birds do you find in the text? Comb through it, looking for these natural references; then explore their significance. How do they deepen your understanding of the play?

3. Do some research into Elizabethan theater design; then discuss how you would stage each scene of *A Midsummer Night's Dream*. You might also want to view the 1999 film version of the play or a live theater production and evaluate their scene production. Do you agree with the choices made? How does scenery used alter or confirm your interpretation of the play?

4. *A Midsummer Night's Dream* was written at about the same time as *Romeo and Juliet*. Compare and contrast the representation of adolescent love in the two plays.

5. Create a collage or painting of this play and then write a statement about your artistic choices. What colors, textures, or images helped you best capture the mood of the drama? What were you forced to leave out?

6. Many listservs and Internet discussion forums are dedicated to discussions of Shakespeare in general and this play in particular (check out the CliffsNotes Resource Center for examples). Join one or more of these groups in order to enhance your understanding of the play.

CliffsNotes Resource Center

The learning doesn't need to stop here. CliffsNotes Resource Center shows you the best of the best—links to the best information in print and online about the author and/or related works. And don't think that this is all we've prepared for you; we've put all kinds of pertinent information at www.cliffsnotes.com. Look for all the terrific resources at your favorite bookstore or local library and on the Internet. When you're online, make your first stop www.cliffsnotes.com where you'll find more incredibly useful information about *A Midsummer Night's Dream*.

Books

This CliffsNotes book provides a meaningful interpretation of *A Midsummer Night's Dream*. If you are looking for information about the author and/or related works, check out these other publications:

Bulfinch's Greek and Roman Mythology: The Age of Fable, by Thomas Bulfinch, provides useful background information on many of the myths referred to in the play. New York: Dover, 2000.

A Midsummer Night's Dream: Critical Essays, edited by Dorothea Kehler. This collection of essays reviews the critical and performance history of the play. It also offers a variety of essays utilizing cutting-edge critical theories such as feminism and deconstruction. New York: Garland, 1998.

A Midsummer Night's Dream: Texts and Contexts, edited by Gail Kern Paster and Skiles Howard. Part of the Bedford Shakespeare Series, this guide reprints the Bevington edition of the play, along with four sets of primary documents and illustrations. The primary texts offer a context for understanding the play's treatment of popular and royal festivity, marriage expectations, the supernatural, and the position of women within early modern culture. Boston: Bedford/St. Martin's, 1999.

Our Moonlight Revels: A Midsummer Night's Dream in the Theatre (Studies in Theatre History and Culture), by Gary Jay Williams. This book offers a carefully detailed and beautifully illustrated history of the play. It covers 400 years of key productions of this drama in Europe, the United States, and Canda, and analyzes important opera, dance, and film adaptations. Iowa City: University of Iowa Press, 1997.

It's easy to find books published by Wiley Publishing, Inc. You'll find them in your favorite bookstores (on the Internet and at a store near you). We also have three Web sites that you can use to read about all the books we publish:

- www.cliffsnotes.com
- www.dummies.com
- www.wiley.com

Internet

Check out these Web resources for more information about William Shakespeare and *A Midsummer Night's Dream*:

A Midsummer Night's Dream **Port**, www.starbuck.com/ shakespeare/AMidsummerhall/wwwboard.html—This site offers students the opportunity to join a light-hearted discussion of the play. There's also a live recitation chat for anyone looking to join a real time discussion of the drama.

Enjoying *A Midsummer Night's Dream,* www.pathguy.com/ mnd.htm—Created by Ed Friedlander, this site is appropriate for both students and adults approaching the play for the first time. The site provides interesting facts and background on the plot and characters, along with analysis of a few integral themes (for example, the importance of dreams and paradox).

Mythology in *A Midsummer Night's Dream,* quarles.unbc.edu/ midsummer/mythintro.html—Check out this site to discover background information on all of the mythological references (Greek, Roman, and Celtic) in the play.

Surfing with the Bard: *A Midsummer Night's Dream* **Guide**, www.ulen.com/shakespeare/plays/mnd/mnd_guide .

html—This Web site provides an excellent introduction to the play. It includes a summary, study questions, an annotated version of the text, and links and photos from several productions. What differentiates this site from others, though, is a downloadable study guide, created by Don Stoneman, that the producers of the site call a "must-have resource for teachers, students and enthusiasts."

Next time you're on the Internet, don't forget to drop by www. cliffsnotes.com. We created an online Resource Center that you can use today, tomorrow, and beyond.

Films and Other Recordings

Check out these films for an older and a more modern production of *A Midsummer Night's Dream*:

A Midsummer Night's Dream, Warner Home Video, 1935. Directed by William Dieterle and Max Reinhardt and starring James Cagney, Dick Powell, Olivia de Havilland. An opulent Hollywood production of the play, this production features the music of Felix Mendolssohn. It is also Olivia de Havilland's film debut and received an Academy Award nomination for Best Picture.

A Midsummer Night's Dream, Twentieth Century Fox, 1999. Directed by Michael Hoffman and starring Kevin Kline, Michelle Pfeiffer, Rupert Everett, Stanley Tucci, and Calista Flockhart. For a review of this film consult the essay "A Tedious Brief Review of Michael Hoffman's *A Midsummer Night's Dream*" in the "Critical Essays" section of this book.

Essays

Following are some essays that you may find interesting in your study of Shakespeare's *A Midsummer Night's Dream*:

DENT, ROBERT W. "Imagination in *A Midsummer Night's Dream*." *Shakespeare Quarterly* 15.2 (1964): 115–129. Dent believes that the most important unifying element of the play is the contrasting role of imagination in love and in art. According to the logic of the play, imagination in love operates in defiance of reason, often creating beauty where none exists. Poetry, on the other hand, offers a universally acceptable vision of beauty.

HOWARD, SKILES. "Hands, Feet, and Bottoms: Decentering the Cosmic Dance in *A Midsummer Night's Dream*." *Shakespeare Quarterly* 44.3 (1993): 325–342. Our understanding of the dances in Shakespeare's plays is often based on the idea of the cosmic dance, an element of elite culture that viewed the social dancing of the courts as an imitation of heavenly motions. But dancing in Shakespeare also had popular folk elements. Howard analyzes the various dances in this play, finding that both cosmic and popular dances are present.

MONTROSE, LOUIS ADRIAN. "Shaping Fantasies: Figurations of Gender and Power in Elizabethan Culture." *Representations* 1.2 (1983): 61–94. Examines the interplay between representations of gender and power in a society in which men have all of the authority. It also considers the dialectical nature of cultural representations, in which plays such as *A Midsummer Night's Dream* simultaneously create and reflect certain cultural ideas.

OLSON, PAUL A. "*A Midsummer Night's Dream* and the Meaning of Court Marriage." *ELH* 24.2 (1957): 95–119. Although *A Midsummer Night's Dream* is often viewed as a lightweight play, Olson argues it is more than a trivial dream. Supposedly written to be performed at a nobleman's wedding, this drama offers a sophisticated philosophy of the nature of love. First, Olson's essay considers the importance of festival drama and marriage in the Renaissance. He then argues that the symbol, structure, and theme of the play together provide a coherent picture of traditional marriage.

Send Us Your Favorite Tips

In your quest for knowledge, have you ever experienced that sublime moment when you figure out a trick that saves time or trouble? Perhaps you realized you were taking ten steps to accomplish something that could have taken two. Or you found a little-known workaround that achieved great results. If you've discovered a useful resource that gave you insight into or helped you understand *A Midsummer Night's Dream*, and you'd like to share it, the CliffsNotes staff would love to hear from you. Go to our Web site at www.cliffsnotes.com and click the Talk to Us button. If we select your tip, we may publish it as part of CliffsNotes Daily, our exciting, free e-mail newsletter. To find out more or to subscribe to a newsletter, go to on the Web.

Index